D0846089

WITHDRAWN

# Democratic Temperament

# American Political Thought

*Edited by*
*Wilson Carey McWilliams & Lance Banning*

# Democratic Temperament

## The Legacy of William James

*Joshua I. Miller*

*University Press of Kansas*

© 1997 by the University Press of Kansas
All rights reserved

Published by the University Press of Kansas (Lawrence, Kansas 66049), which was organized by the Kansas Board of Regents and is operated and funded by Emporia State University, Fort Hays State University, Kansas State University, Pittsburg State University, the University of Kansas, and Wichita State University

Library of Congress Cataloging-in-Publication Data

Miller, Joshua (Joshua I.)
Democratic temperament : the legacy of William James / Joshua
I. Miller.
p. cm. — (American political thought)
Includes bibliographical references and index.
ISBN 0-7006-0831-1 (alk. paper)
1. James, William, 1842–1910—Contributions in political science.
2. Democracy. I. Title. II. Series.
JC213.J35M56 1997
320′.092—dc21 96-51864

British Library Cataloguing in Publication Data is available.

Printed in the United States of America

10 9 8 7 6 5 4 3 2 1

The paper used in this publication meets the minimum requirements of the American National Standard for Permanence of Paper for Printed Library Materials Z39.48-1984.

*To my grandmother Ruth L. Weisbach,*
*and to my father, mother, brother, and sister:*
*Jay, Joyce, Adam, and Rebecca Miller*

# CONTENTS

# FOREWORD

If Alexis de Tocqueville is to be believed, Americans of the Jacksonian era were pragmatists well before there were philosophers of pragmatism. In *Democracy in America* he observed that in the United States, "the purely practical side of science" was energetically developed but that "hardly anyone" was concerned with "the essentially theoretical and abstract side" of knowledge (*Democracy in America*, ed. J. P. Mayer and trans. George Lawrence [Garden City, N.Y.: Anchor edition, Doubleday, 1969], 460). Tocqueville was suggesting what many later commentators would echo, that pragmatism, with its emphasis upon an experimental approach to virtually everything, from morals and religion to politics and economy, presupposed a setting sufficiently spacious, richly endowed, and sparsely populated to support a general culture of trial and error and to dismiss as abstruse any speculation that seemed unpromising in immediate payoff. To invoke Tocqueville once more, America was the land where one could always correct one's mistakes.

Arguably, during much of the twentieth century pragmatism was widely viewed by American philosophers and political theorists as the modern, even the postmodern, version of democratic theory. John Dewey, in particular, popularized the notion that pragmatism or, in his formulation, "instrumentalism," stood for the application of scientific method to social problems. Understood pragmatically, democracy was the political equivalent of, or at least the analogue to, scientific method. Its politics was said to be characteristically experimental since a free political life meant not being bound by the dogmas of the past or deference to wealth and privilege. In the manner of a scientist the democrat depended upon the free and open exchange of ideas—to identify problems, to deliberate over the proper solutions, and to compare their relative consequences. And if one approach failed, try another.

Today, the United States no longer seems quite as capacious as the founders of pragmatism assumed. Our borders are tightly policed, and immigrants are widely regarded as a public burden. And the skeletal remains of old forests and of vacant high-rise, low-cost housing developments suggest that, contra Tocqueville, the margin for corrigible mistakes has narrowed. There are also other causes at work that make the flexible politics presupposed by the theory of pragmatism questionable and tend to render that theory more of an acquired taste than a national instinct.

Ironically, those causes are related to the deliberate cultivation—or perhaps overcultivation—of two basic principles of pragmatism: the supreme importance of encouraging the growth of the natural sciences, and especially their practical applications, and of applying a rational method (analogous to the experimental methods employed by scientists) to the solution of social problems. Contemporary science is, in the popular phrase, "big science," requiring considerable financial resources—public and corporate—as well as huge research installations and a large and steady supply of highly trained scientists. Science is integrated into both the corporate economy and the structure of government. Which is to say, to a large extent, big science is bureaucratized rather than autonomous. At the same time, the sciences, whether big or not, have ceased to be viewed as the unambiguous ideal they had been for the founders of pragmatism. Significantly, today's neopragmatists, for the most part, have simply dropped science.

A comparable disillusionment has emerged out of the efforts to define and solve social problems by means of government action. Rapidly changing, highly integrated societies appear to have an infinite capacity for generating social problems. For more than a half century the main political response has been the attempt to resolve problems by the actions of federal and state governments, which meant enlarging the size and power of governments and, largely unnoticed, conceiving of political action as engagement in problem-solving by means of "policy." Once action was equated with problem solving through policy formulation, the next development seemed to follow naturally. Ever since the New Deal the idea of action-as-policy has been touted as the governmental version of scientific method. The fields of application have been virtually endless, from economic policy to immigration policy, from defense policy to environmental policy. A policy requires that a problem, say, toxic waste disposal, be defined and delimited so it is analyzable by formal methods that typically claim to be following "rigorous," i.e., scientific, ways of thinking. The methods may take a variety of forms: rational choice and cost-benefit analysis are among the more familiar ones. But the abstract character of the methods of analysis has also proved congenial to big government because they are readily adaptable to bureaucratic modes of action such as regulation or rule-making. Typically, bureaucracies attempt to set a uniform rule for a large number of circumstances or cases that, in fact, display widely varying local differences.

As of this moment, the principal critics of bureaucratic action are and have been business spokesmen, opponents of welfare programs, leaders of the so-called militia movement, and defenders of property rights. What may be among the stakes in this challenge is the privatization of action. The response to the controversy on the part of political leaders, federal and state, has been to treat it as a problem of administration that calls for "reinventing government" by reducing its size, scope, and costs. Unfortunately, action itself remains firmly bureaucratized.

To the dilemma of the bureaucratization of political action versus the privatization of action, Joshua Miller's *Democratic Temperament* offers a fresh and important alternative. He has undertaken to retrieve the notion of political action and restate it within the context of a radical democratic conception of politics. He rejects the antipolitical direction and hyper-individualism of the privatizers in favor of seeking common and shared values through democratic forms of action based on respect, trust, and equality. But he also defends the idea of smaller scales of action than those represented even by reinvented government. His arguments are developed by using William James's pragmatic conception of action as a starting point. Although Miller is careful to state fairly, though not uncritically, various Jamesian positions, his main concern is to address some hard contemporary questions about democracy and the meaning of citizen action. He has retained the openness, verve, and directness of James as well as James's delight in human differences and impatience with pretense. A reader who enjoys watching theory at work on questions that are both serious and immediate will greatly profit from these pages.

Sheldon Wolin
Whale Gulch, Mendocino

# PREFACE

It is no small burden to try to bring someone new into theory's conversation about politics. "No room! No room!" Epic theorists—Plato, Aristotle, Machiavelli, Rousseau, Hobbes, Locke, Mill, and Marx—take up a lot of space at the table, and other European giants—Kant, Hegel, Nietzsche, Heidegger, Benjamin, Foucault, Habermas—also command positions. Some Americans occupy seats, despite the supercilious glances of the Europeans: Winthrop, Jefferson, John Adams, Paine, Madison, Hamilton, Calhoun, Lincoln, Henry Adams, John Dewey, Randolph Bourne, Jane Addams, Martin Luther King, Jr., and Hannah Arendt. Should James have a place at theory's table?

Convincing theorists that William James was a significant political thinker will certainly take work. One night at a political science convention, I was hoping to impress a theorist over a drink. She was jazzed about a new study group on postmodernism at her university. "What are you working on?," she asked.

"I study American political thought, and I'm doing a book on William James."

"William James? Didn't he write *The Turn of the Screw?*"

"No, that was his brother, Henry. William was a psychologist and philosopher who lived from 1842 to 1910. He was the author of *Pragmatism;* his *Principles of Psychology* used to be the standard textbook in psychology courses throughout the country; he was America's preeminent philosopher at the end of the nineteenth century. The *New York Times* once published a front page interview with him about his ideas. I'm trying to draw out the implications of his thinking for political theory."

"That's interesting," she sighed. After a few minutes of conversation on other topics, she asked me again what I was working on.

"William James." I realized that romance was a dimming possibility.

"Yes, you said that. That's not very postmodern, is it?"

I could have replied that James actually was postmodern in crucial ways. Although not denying the existence of truth or God, he rejected the idea that they can be known with any certainty. He believed that convictions and causes are risky choices whose veracity cannot be guaranteed by reference to an external standard. The link between James and postmodernism has been made explicit by Richard Rorty, a liberal postmodernist philosopher who has invoked James and pragmatism as a direct antecedent of his argument for the benefits of antifoundationalism, which is the recognition that one's truths do not rest on objective grounding. And there are close similarities between James and political theorist William Connolly's case for ambiguity and "agonistic democracy." The postmodernists' preoccupations with contingency, truth, belief, difference, and action were at the heart of James's concerns.

I could have told her that the perverse nature of contemporary political life makes listening to James particularly urgent. Public conversation about politics has become strikingly uncivil. Campaigns are built on attack ads, which everyone deplores while the ads remain effective. Generosity toward opponents is defined as weakness. Every scrap of personal failing, mistaken utterance, or controversial vote is used as a weapon to destroy one's adversary. Moderates on abortion are denounced as baby killers, opponents of the death penalty are said to be soft on crime, and to suggest that taxes need to be raised or that the poor need more help is political suicide. Advocates of every position claim the moral high ground and denounce those who disagree as enemies of the people. In the aftermath of the Civil War, James asked how proponents of various causes could act without trying to demolish, conquer, or demonize the other side.

I should have told my friend that if she shared with many postmodernists a faith in radical democracy, she should study James's theories of action and mutual respect, because if she happened to wonder why people take part in politics and asked if the "typical" motivation for action is compatible with regard for opponents, she could find in James illumination of the complexities of democratic political consciousness. I might have summed up by saying that James's great contribution to political theory is his comprehension of the political actor's psychology. But that night in the bar, having abandoned hope, I mentioned none of this. I could not yet quickly convey what mattered in James's thought.

I began to study James without knowing what I was looking for in his work. Wilson Carey McWilliams proposed to me that the contributions to American political thought of a number of philosophers, including Royce, James, and Santayana, might be more fully articulated. I offered to write on James because I knew him to be a localist and a great writer, even though I distrusted pragmatism as the potential enemy of visionary, i.e., radical politics.

In this record of my engagement with James, I have attempted to create a work of political theory rather than an intellectual history. As I understand theory's task, it is to address contemporary political problems by examining how previous theorists have grappled with similar issues. I have tried here to bring James into the political dialogue of the present by articulating his ideas concerning democratic action. By explicating, criticizing, and meditating on James, I develop my own ideas about issues facing democracy and democrats today. Although taking James as my focal point, I am attending to contemporary problems that preoccupy theorists. Therefore, I am quite selective in the themes that I treat in James's thought, focusing on the themes that concern significant issues in democratic theory and practice.

At the heart of the book is James's description of the democratic temperament, which I take to be a healthy corrective to the distemper that characterizes so much of politics today. The democratic temperament includes a willingness to act, placing the public good ahead of private comfort, generosity toward one's opponents, and a nearly universal respect— which, for James, included women, African Americans, workers, inhabitants of the Third World, and even white members of the middle and upper classes.

I could have written a more empirical book in which I used primarily historical and contemporary examples of democratic politics to illustrate James's theory of democratic temperament, describing the members and leaders of unions, parties, cause organizations, and experiments in egalitarian or consensual decision making. I might have studied the biographies of politicians and activists, perhaps even interviewing them about their worldviews and self-understandings to see if they corresponded to James's categories. Instead of following either of those approaches, in writing about James on political consciousness I have drawn on my own political experiences, those I have witnessed, and those about which I have read.

My political education began at home. My father was a trade union organizer and business agent before assuming a leadership role in the peace and civil rights movements. Later he became a career official of the American Civil Liberties Union. My mother studied labor education in graduate school at the University of Chicago before becoming an education director and a social services director, first in the Midwest and then nationally, for the Amalgamated Clothing and Textile Workers Union. She was one of the founders of the Coalition of Labor Union Women, serving for many years as its president, and was the first woman to sit on the executive board of the AFL-CIO. Through my parents, I met many people whose lives are devoted to social change. I have had some political experiences of my own, as a participant in the antiwar movement as a high school student and, after college, as a community organizer for two years in the South. My sister, Rebecca, is the political director of 1199, the National Health and Human Service Employees Union.

Perhaps because of this family background, when I write about politics I usually am thinking about visionaries and activists of movements and organizations, and sometimes public officials, who work to bring about major changes in the political order. Abraham Lincoln, Ida B. Wells, Jane Addams, Tom Hayden, Martin Luther King, Jr., and John Lewis are often on my mind. These men and women are the political equivalents of James's "saints" described in his *Varieties of Religious Experience*. My preoccupation with transformative politics is consonant with James's religious, moral, and political concerns. Although he sometimes emphasized the preservation of American institutions, he was equally interested in how societies are radically altered and in the mental outlook of the people who lead society through those changes.

My first debt of gratitude in writing this book is to Carey McWilliams, one of the most prominent political theorists in the United States. We had many helpful conversations about James, and the book is much stronger because of his skill and insight in reviewing the manuscript. I incorporated many of his ideas into the final version, and I am grateful to Carey and to

Fred Woodward, director of the University Press of Kansas, for their warmth and enthusiasm for this project.

I began by being a bit unnerved about discussing James's thought without knowing my mentors' estimation of him; they never lectured on James. Then I took some pride in my intellectual independence. As Flannery O'Connor wrote in a letter, "I keep clear of Faulkner so my own little boat won't get swamped." Without commenting on the draft chapters of the manuscript I sent them, they still offered crucial advice. John Schaar, professor of political theory at the University of California, Santa Cruz, advised me not to jump on the bandwagon of the pragmatism revival by arguing primarily with contemporary commentators but to instead face James directly. In our several conversations about the book, Sheldon Wolin, my former graduate adviser in Princeton's political philosophy program, urged me to look at the historical forces that led James to theoretical paradoxes and insisted that a conventional book about James would not be worth writing.

After nearly six years of work, I had completed what I assumed was the final substantive draft of this book. At that point, Wolin offered me his suggestions for revising the manuscript. This act of remarkable generosity took Wolin away from his own writing projects to dictate several hours of comments on microcassettes, which I transcribed to nearly twenty single-spaced pages of invaluable ideas for revision and numerous insights into the theoretical issues with which I was wrestling. He reminded me of the history of those issues in the tradition of political theory and proffered alternative interpretations of James. Fred Woodward wisely allowed me just three months to make revisions. How to incorporate and properly credit Wolin's work became a dilemma. I have included many of his remarks in the text and notes and cited them as his; in other places, I have silently (and more traditionally) integrated his editorial recommendations into the text. I wished to share his insights with the reader, and I believe this unusual inclusion of commentary into the text will make for interesting reading. It was a pleasure to work with Wolin on the book, and I am grateful for his efforts.

I have also benefited from the intelligent critiques of various chapters by Charles Hersch, Brian Weiner, Elaine Thomas, Janet Ewald, Laurie Maffly-Kipp, Ernst Manasse, Casey Blake, Romand Coles, Ingrid Creppell, and Richard Rorty. I had no intention of writing a chapter on James and gender until I fell under the influence of a seminar on race and gender at the National Humanities Center in 1993–1994. At the last meeting of the seminar I presented my chapter and received extraordinarily helpful comments from Paula Giddings, Evelyn Brooks Higginbotham, Claudia Koonz, Luise White, Judith Bennett, John Thompson, Gary Shapiro, and Mark Mazower.

My teacher, the late Maurice Natanson, and my friends Nicholas Xenos and Wendy Brown provided important counsel on the writing and publication of this book. I delivered an early version of the chapter on education as a Jones Lecture, "Democratic Pedagogy," at Lafayette College in spring 1993 and presented another to the Political Science Club at North Carolina State University in fall 1994. I also profited from discussions with students and faculty at the University of Texas, Austin, and Tulane University as well as from panels of the American Political Science Association and the Western Political Science Association. Students in my spring 1995 graduate seminar on pragmatism and politics in the Political Science Department at Rutgers University helped me to clarify my ideas, as did the members of my senior seminar on democratic action at Lafayette College in fall 1994.

Completion of this book depended upon public funding for the humanities, and I am very grateful to the National Endowment for Humanities for supporting a revivifying year at the National Humanities Center in Research Triangle Park, North Carolina, during which most of this book was written. Every member of the center's administration and staff, from the director to the engineer, believes in the cause of scholarship and does everything possible to make a Fellow's stay productive and pleasurable. Also, Lafayette College generously granted me a sabbatical, a summer research fellowship, and student research assistance. Nicole Piccione proved to be an excellent copyeditor, and Terese Heidenwolf and Vaswati Sinha of Skillman Library's Reference Department solved many bibliographic problems for me. I did my own typing and printing, but Lafayette's Computing Services Department—including its former director Les Lloyd, Tracy Logan, Lori Young, and students Diane Lorenzo and Bridget Solimeno—provided me with the equipment I needed and patiently solved many mysteries of its use. A gift from my grandmother allowed me to acquire the other tools I needed to complete the book.

I gratefully acknowledge permission from Kluwer Academic Publishers to reprint "Truth in the Experience of Political Actors," an early version of Chapters 1 and 4, that appears in *The Prism of the Self: Philosophical Essays in Honor of Maurice Natanson*, ed. Steven Galt Crowell (1995).

At the conclusion of the race and gender seminar, Judith Bennett declared, "I'm sure that we all like William James more than we did before we read Josh's paper." I was pleased by her remark, but persuading readers to like James is not my goal; my primary aim is to stimulate the reader's thinking about the issues concerning democratic action raised in the various chapters. Nevertheless, it would be good if more people read James. I can attest to the fact that a serious engagement with James is an intellectually pleasurable and transformative experience.

# Introduction

## I

Before turning to James's explicit ideas about democratic action, I must establish the fact that he had political interests, because treating James as a theorist, or even as a thinker with serious political concerns, may seem strange to people familiar with his traditional identities as a philosopher, psychologist, and interpreter of religious experience. It has been frequently asserted that he was a radical individualist, with no interest in politics,[1] and discussions of pragmatism's political implications usually turn quickly from James to Dewey.[2] At the same time, critics characterize James as a democrat, an egalitarian, and a localist before passing on to other themes in his work. More recent commentators, however, especially George Cotkin and Deborah J. Coon, have shown that James's lack of interest and insight into politics has been exaggerated.[3]

Admittedly, his attention to the tradition of political theory was not comparable to his devotion to philosophy, psychology, and the supernatural, but James was not ignorant of that tradition. He knew and criticized Plato, Hegel, and Nietzsche. His *Principles of Psychology* frequently cites Hobbes's *Leviathan*, and he acknowledged the influences of John Stuart Mill, *Nation* editor E. L. Godkin, and Tolstoy on his political thinking.[4] It is thus no surprise that James often called himself a "liberal." One can presume that as a well-educated Harvard professor and a godson of Ralph Waldo Emerson, James was steeped in the classic texts of American political thought. His student Santayana thought that James's devotion to the principles of the Declaration of Independence was at the heart of his "naive" anti-imperialism.[5]

Much of James's writing is implicitly related to politics. He had a Puritan commitment to moral action, i.e., to combating evil in order to reshape the world according to a vision of justice. James believed that God

1

exists and is on the side of good, but he also believed that God offers no salvation if people do not struggle to save themselves. To depoliticize this theme in James's work reflects an overly narrow definition of politics rather than its true place in James's thought. There is no reason to restrict James's reflections on action to private life since he made clear that he did not sharply distinguish between public and private action. In *The Will to Believe*, James was concerned with the philosophical and psychological bases for acting when faith in absolute truth has been shaken. The essays "Great Men and Their Environment" and "The Moral Philosopher and the Moral Life" can be read as descriptions of the psychological and ethical dilemmas of a person who wants to transform institutions and ideas.[6] In *Varieties of Religious Experience,* James identified radical political actors with the religious activists he studies in the book: "The Utopian dreams of social justice in which many contemporary socialists and anarchists indulge are, in spite of their impracticability and non-adaptation to present environmental conditions, analogous to the saints' belief in an existent kingdom of heaven."[7]

James expressly discussed such political themes as action, equality, citizenship, obstacles to respect among individuals and communities, materialism, and war in his essays "A Certain Blindness in Human Beings," "What Makes a Life Significant," and "The Moral Equivalent of War" and in his speeches "Robert Gould Shaw" and "Remarks at the Peace Banquet." Although he did not pay sufficient attention, from the standpoint of political theory, to institutions, economics, or power, his insights into psychology and religion can be applied to political experience. I do not claim that his primary concern was politics, but the political dimension of his work has been insufficiently acknowledged and studied.

In this book, I do not attempt to address all aspects of James's political thinking but instead focus on the theme of democracy. By "democracy," I usually mean radical or participatory democracy and thus distinguish democracy from two terms with which it is commonly associated, "liberalism" and "representation." Many readers distrust radical democracy with its stress upon citizen power, action, equality, and community. They prefer liberalism that, in its ideal form, is embodied in a benign and limited centralized authority which protects individual rights and represents the people's true interests. Radical democrats do not repudiate the ideals of individual rights and a government that rules in the public interest, but they emphasize equality of power; direct participation of citizens in decision making, both in politics and in civil society; and mutual respect for the diverse members of the community. As one who believes in participatory democracy, my political ideas differ from James's: he was not consistently a radical democrat, although much of his thought is compatible with radical democracy. In this book, I translate James's thinking into the language of democratic politics, not only interpreting him to be a theorist of action but also exploring the complexities of that theory.

Students of politics should be interested in James because he speaks to the paradoxical condition of modern political existence: widespread withdrawal from public life combined with fanatic action. James lived through the Civil War and wrote his major works during the era of massive immigration from Europe, the building of the railroads, the escalation of American imperialism, the Populist movement, the campaign for women's suffrage, the Haymarket riot, and violent struggles between labor and management. Reconstruction was dismantled while lynching became common, the Ku Klux Klan was formed, Jim Crow laws were passed, and, in response, a nascent civil rights movement took shape.[8] Nonviolent resolution of domestic and international conflicts seemed a remote possibility. Yet, even in this period of change, James and other intellectuals were anxious about a lack of reasonable political action.[9] The national government had become corrupt after the Civil War, and after the defeat of the Populist party in 1898, citizens began to withdraw from national politics.[10] Political scientist W. Y. P. Elliott wrote that

the twentieth century began with a fear of the monstrous complexity with which it was faced hanging in the air like a heavy pall. Life had lost forever, men seemed to think, the poetic simplicity and untroubled confidence with which the youth of Western civilization had faced its problems. Eucken said of this time . . . : "paralyzing doubt saps the vitality of our age. We see a clear proof of this in the fact that with all our achievements and unremitting progress we are not really happy. . . ." The prophet of this period is old Henry Adams.[11]

James believed resignation to be a danger to democracy, and even today passivity remains a formidable obstacle to the recovery of democratic politics. In *The Prince,* Machiavelli depicted a popular attitude like the one James saw in the United States in the late 1800s and one that remains widespread:

> It is not unknown to me that many have held, and still hold, the opinion that the things of this world are, in a manner, controlled by Fortune and by God, that men with their wisdom cannot control them, and that, on the contrary, men can have no remedy whatsoever for them; and for this reason they might judge that they need not sweat much over such matters but let them be governed by fate. This opinion has been more strongly held in our own times because of the great variation of affairs that has been observed and that is being observed every day which is beyond all human conjecture.[12]

From the standpoint of the people who are acquiescent, God, the government, late capitalism, or any power except themselves and their neighbors shapes reality and controls events; human beings are helpless to do more than accommodate to the direction of force. Seeing no hope for political change, many citizens focus on themselves (the private life of self, friends, family, work, body, spirit, psyche, pleasures) or turn their attention from this world to the next.

James challenged those elements of American political culture that encourage compliance, particularly education and the rise of large-scale institutions.[13] Even today most conflicts are not resolved democratically; usually one person or a small group decides and then gives orders to subordinates. Despite our nation's professed commitment to democracy, the bureaucratic, hierarchical model is assumed to be natural, efficient, just, and conducive to productivity, and this model has been adopted by most corporations, families, colleges and universities, and even social change organizations. Because challenging authority is risky, most citizens obey the people who have power over them, even when they strongly disagree with their actions or beliefs, both because they fear the penalties of resistance and because they have come to accept inequality as natural. From the perspective of Jean-Jacques Rousseau, continuous obedience without consent is a system of coercion akin to slavery. One function of leaders and teachers, according to James, is to overcome resignation and initiate action.[14]

As in James's time, the popular alternative to passivity is still moral absolutism. For James, this concept was embodied in the imperialism of Teddy Roosevelt, in American chauvinism, and in the inability of the bourgeoisie and working classes to understand the other's point of view. Today, moral absolutism can be seen in the anti-abortion movement, the religious right, parts of the left, the Nation of Islam, and the campaign to censor books, television, music, art, and film. One fears that acts of political terrorism, such as the bombings of the World Trade Center and the Oklahoma Federal Building and the shootings of doctors and staff members at abortion clinics, will increase. Many groups and individuals act as if they have a direct line to God, condemning their opponents as deluded or deviant; their demands are nonnegotiable. Absolutism is antidemocratic because politics requires recognition of, and negotiation with, opponents; democratic politics implies that people are at least allowed to state their claims and, ideally, to take part in making a decision.[15] Neither passivity in the face of increasing governmental and corporate power nor violence, terrorism, and hatred are harmonious with democracy.

As I explain in Chapter 3, James sought to balance action based on a self-critical faith with tolerance for the causes of others. His concept of "the will to believe" spoke to intellectuals who feared that they could not act legitimately if they could not discover solid external ground (e.g., God's will) or scientific certitude for their causes. According to James, motives for human action are never completely rational, and therefore people should abandon the quest for certainty; if they do so they will be less likely to censure the causes of others.

Democrats today wish to promote, as did James, both principled action and mutual respect among citizens of different viewpoints, races, genders, classes, and religions. James offers, if not a path leading out of resignation and violence, an analysis of the antecedents of those reactions and the difficulties of overcoming them. One finds James to be a critic of imperialism and absolutism and an advocate for esteeming and tolerating diverse cultures. It might not be too strong to say that in this advocacy, James laid the groundwork for the cultural pluralism developed by Randolph Bourne and James's student Horace Kallen.[16]

# II

I will say something now of James's life, but only a little, for I have no wish to contribute to the tradition of subsuming his ideas to his admittedly compelling biography.[17] In his person, James was short, charismatic, and a sharp dresser. In personality, he was humane, lively, and generous, and those qualities are reflected in much of his political thinking. Born in New York City, William was the oldest son of Henry James, Sr., one of the wealthiest men in America and an eccentric writer on literature and religion. Ralph Waldo Emerson was a friend of the elder James and visited his home on Washington Square a few days after William was born. At Emerson's suggestion, Henry David Thoreau also called on Henry James. William's younger brother, Henry, Jr., wrote *The Turn of the Screw, The Bostonians, Portrait of a Lady,* and *What Maisie Knew,* and his invalid sister, Alice, has received attention from feminist scholars for her insightful diary.[18] Two other brothers fought in the Civil War. Wilkinson James, who served under Robert Gould Shaw in the 54th Massachusetts Infantry, a black regiment, was wounded at Fort Wagner. After the war, "Wilky" and Robertson James started a racially integrated farm in Florida, but it failed, largely because of attacks by local racists after they discovered Wilky's connection with Shaw.

In 1860–1861, William James studied painting in Newport, Rhode Island. Abandoning that career at the insistence of his father, he entered Harvard where he studied chemistry and anatomy. In 1863, he began medical school, graduating in 1869; the M.D. was his only degree. He interrupted his training to join a scientific expedition to Brazil and then studied psychology in Germany.

Although William James was a man of prodigious energy and accomplishment, he was afflicted throughout his life with feelings of depression and lethargy. He had a nervous breakdown at twenty-eight, which concluded with the adoption of a new philosophy that posited a pluralistic universe in which convictions are chosen rather than supplied by God. James went on to teach psychology and physiology at Harvard and later became a professor of philosophy at the same institution. His students included Gertrude Stein, W. E. B. Du Bois, Walter Lippmann, Horace Kallen, and Theodore Roosevelt, each of whom had a significant impact on American politics, political theory, or culture. James sought an audience for his ideas that was broader than professional philosophers.[19] After his classic works, the two-volume *Principles of Psychology* and his essays *Will to Believe*, his most prominent books are collections of public lectures: *Talks to Teachers, Varieties of Religious Experience*, and *Pragmatism*.

In the 1890s, James took an increasing interest in politics.[20] In 1895, he protested the United States' role in the crisis connected with the Venezuela boundary dispute and "was henceforth keenly concerned about colonialism, imperialism, international relations, militarism, and America's role in the world scene."[21] He supported the nineteenth-century movement to establish and protect African Americans' civil rights and publicly denounced lynching. He vigorously protested U.S. involvement in the Philippines and in the Spanish-American War.[22] James had a strong interest in defining the public role of the intellectual, and he distinguished theory from action. In a letter to Wincenty Lutoslawski, a Polish Plato scholar and political reformer whom James highly respected, he wrote: "Division of labor is the great thing. You belong to the theoretic sphere as few men do, and you do not belong to the practical sphere. Work out the abstract theory of freedom, and let the close-lipped, iron-willed, hard-hearted men of affairs who exist for that purpose translate it into action. Thus it shall best succeed."[23] In his letters, James defined his vocation variously as philosopher, academic, teacher, and intellectual, yet he believed all of those activities had a public dimension.[24]

# III

In the chapters that follow, I attempt to articulate a coherent democratic theory in James's writings, yet I must also acknowledge his contradictions. He was a pacifist who called for a warlike spirit. He was egalitarian and open to points of view dismissed by most others, but he was also an elitist who called the college-educated an aristocracy and the many "a herd of nullities." The individual was perhaps his central value, but he insisted that people had strong obligations to serve the community. He has been labeled an anarchist because he hated institutions that might restrain creativity and energy and recognized that geniuses were innovators who transgressed existing laws and customs. Yet he also supported the constitutional order and said that punishing lawbreakers was essential to its preservation. He seemed to believe in God but doubted that God could be comprehended. Although asserting that we can never be sure that our values are ultimately true, he often assumed that the liberal reformist values of his circle were true and was convinced that history would eventually remake reality according to those values. The philosophy of pragmatism emphasizes the practical and successful, but James also celebrated idealists, visionaries, and lost causes. He believed in and practiced the scholarly and intellectual life, but he praised action so much—hating ideals that were not acted upon—that he has sometimes been depicted as anti-intellectual. What method of interpretation is appropriate for a thinker with so many contradictions?

It has been said that James's ideas embody that part of Nietzsche that Americans can accept.[25] James's figure of the genius, which I will discuss in Chapters 1 and 5, is reminiscent of Nietzsche's overman. Yet, there is no strain nihilism or misogyny in James, and James wrote, "The sallies of the two German authors [Schopenhauer and Nietzsche] remind one, half the time, of the sick shriekings of two dying rats."[26] James's contradictions, at least, may be comparable to those of Nietzsche, and Karl Jaspers provides a model for interpreting James in his reading of Nietzsche:

> The interpretative study of Nietzsche's thinking thus always requires the gathering together of *all* utterances that relate to a given topic. . . . All statements seem to be annulled by other statements. *Self-contradiction* is the fundamental ingredient in Nietzsche's thought. For nearly every single one of Nietzsche's judgments, one can also find an opposite. He gives the impression of having two opinions about everything. Consequently it is possible to quote Nietzsche at will in support of anything one happens to have in mind.[27]

The method of this book is inspired by Jaspers's recommendation to bring together statements that appear to be contradictory. Virtually every chapter focuses on a paradox in James's thinking. In struggling with each paradox I attempt both to interpret James's "real" intention and to draw out of the paradox something illuminating for politics today, particularly the possibility and problems of reviving democracy.

What are the ambiguities of democratic revival? Leadership is needed if efforts at social change are to succeed, yet leadership itself can overwhelm initiatives on the part of the many. Public opinion can be terribly wrong—supporting demagogues, punishment, sexism, and violence—yet the people must be respected in order to accomplish democratic transformations. Politics should be conducted with gentleness and courtesy, but struggles over power are intensely fought and one seems to need a strong stomach and sufficient aggression to play hardball. Democracy implies mutual respect among people who hold contrary opinions and who battle for conflicting gains, yet the very faith or self-interest that motivates political action makes it difficult to tolerate the opposition. Tolerance probably requires a feeling of commonality, a sense that even though we disagree we are bound by common values or a country. The question then arises, Is all commonality coercive? If education is necessary to develop a "democratic temperament," can that temperament be fostered by an education that contains significant elements of elitism, hierarchy, and discipline? These questions are at the heart of democratic politics and at the center of James's political thought.

*Chapter 1*

# Models of Action

William James broke with the liberal tradition in which political action has held a secondary place. In Hobbes's *Leviathan* and Locke's *Second Treatise on Government* individuals turn their power over to the sovereign, even if they retain the right to revolution, to be used only in extraordinary circumstances. Neither Hobbes nor Locke had much good to say about ordinary citizen action.[1] The Federalists pejoratively linked nongovernmental initiatives with selfish and frenzied factions. The Constitution sanctions peaceable assembly and petition of the government for redress of grievances but does not institutionalize participation other than voting. In the late nineteenth century, the English theorist Herbert Spencer (1820–1903) developed a social Darwinism that disavowed the need for government in favor of individualism and "voluntary social cooperation." The only legitimate purposes for cooperation, Spencer avowed, were war and the protection of persons and property. He made virtually no mention of direct action or public decision making in communities, organizations, or the nation.[2] In the United States, conservative sociologist and social Darwinist William Graham Sumner rejected the idea that classes have obligations toward one another and derided political reform as "the absurd attempt to make the world over."[3]

Before elaborating James's alternative assessment of action, I offer this summary of his theory: he celebrated action, including political action; his advocacy of popular action is a democratic element of his thought that undermines its elitist elements; and he envisioned several models of action, some more democratic than others. Despite his professed individualism, James believed that people are connected to their communities and have obligations both to their fellow citizens and to past and future generations. The historical context for James's writings included the intensely bitter public clashes of the Civil War, the Spanish-American War, and racial and class struggles, so that for James to commend conflict took no small amount of courage.

10

# I

In his most democratic thinking, James identified action with personal and political health; it suggested freedom and vitality.[4] For James, action implied more than mere voting behavior, the expression of preferences, and the pursuit of self-interest. Action is the development of one's potential in the service of a cause greater than oneself; it is thus simultaneously self-fulfillment and self-sacrifice. Respect for action makes James an ally of democracy, which is defined by citizen action rather than constitutions and institutions.[5]

In designing the United States Constitution, the Federalists tried to rein in popular participation and separate it from public power.[6] They understood passion to have a dynamic character that, if stirred, makes citizens difficult to control. In *Federalist* 6, Hamilton put the rhetorical question, "Are not popular assemblies frequently subject to the impulses of rage, resentment, jealousy, avarice, and of other irregular and violent propensities?" and Madison disparagingly connected democracy and passion in *Federalist* 10:

> A pure Democracy, by which I mean, a Society, consisting of a small number of citizens, who assemble and administer the Government in person, can admit of no cure for the mischiefs of faction. A common passion or interest will, in almost every case, be felt by a majority of the whole. . . . Hence it is that such Democracies have ever been spectacles of turbulence and contention; have ever been found incompatible with personal security or the rights of property; and have in general been as short in their lives as they have been violent in their deaths.[7]

Whereas the Federalists thought that participation was dangerous because it resulted in passion and partisanship, James encouraged participation precisely because it elicited passion from the citizens. James averred, in oddly archaic language, that there will be change

> even in this shrunken and enfeebled generation. . . . Battles and defeats will occur, the victors will be glorified and the vanquished dishonored just as in the brave days of yore, the human heart still with-

drawing itself from the much it has in safe possession, and concentrating all its passion upon those evanescent possibilities of fact which still quiver in fate's scale.[8]

For James, moral action required personal commitment. "We find such persons in every age, passionately flinging themselves upon their sense of the goodness of life, in spite of the hardships of their own condition."[9] In his *Talks to Teachers,* James endorsed the "popular belief" that "estimate[s] the worth of a man's mental processes by their effects upon his practical life." In this view,

> the man of contemplation would be treated as only half a human being, passion and practical resource would become once more glories of our race, a concrete victory over this earth's outward powers of darkness would appear an equivalent for any amount of passive spiritual culture, and conduct would remain as the test of every education worthy of the name.[10]

In "The Moral Equivalent of War," James called for the peaceful use of "civic passion" for which people would "lay down their persons and their wealth" to create a community of which citizens could be proud rather than one in which many are subject to unrelieved "toil and pain and hardness and inferiority" while others lead lives of ease.[11] This civic passion would include heroism, endurance, and discipline, not, as it might have for Teddy Roosevelt, military conquest or domination.

James recognized the problematic dimension of passion: people have an instinct for war that demagogic politicians and the press can manipulate for destructive ends.[12] When the public supported war with Spain, James blamed Congress and the press—James hated Hearst's yellow journalism—for stirring up popular emotions, and he perceived the esteeming of fervor for its own sake to be an upper-class characteristic.[13] Unlike the Federalists, James did not see passion as the peculiar problem of the masses.

> Whatever happens, in any event, will happen not as the result of any particular reason, but as the result of passion, and of certain watchwords that nations have learned habitually to obey. We have some pretty good ones of the latter sort, which will make for reason. But the

*great* passion undeniably now is the passion for *adventure*. . . . And, after all, has n't the spirit of the life of all the great generals and rulers and aristocracies always been the spirit of sport carried to its supreme expression? Civilization, properly so-called, might well be termed the organization of all those functions that resist the mere excitement of sport.[14]

Especially in the face of enthusiasm for war and imperialism, James endorsed the representative institutions of the Constitution, the principle of checks and balances, and the cooler thinking of intellectuals as restraints on popular rages. Passion is, however, an inexorable force in politics, according to James, and therefore he did not seek to eliminate it but to channel it into public-spirited activity of the type described in "The Moral Equivalent of War."[15] For James, political conflict, ideally legal and nonviolent, connotes not anarchy but moral courage, resistance to large, centralized institutions, and the necessary, if painful, path to progress.[16] Conflict expresses vitality, catharsis, and concern for the common good.[17]

For James, action is good in itself, not only as a means to an end; psychological, moral, and even material benefits come as much from striving to realize an ideal as from attaining it.[18] Open struggle is better for a body politic than resignation or suppression of discontent, which, if stifled, can lead to violent eruptions. James put a positive spin on the fierce presidential election of 1896: "Our political crisis is over, but the hard times still endure. . . . I doubt, notwithstanding certain appearances, whether the country was ever morally in as sound a state as it is now, after all this discussion."[19] He had expressed the same sentiment ten years earlier in a letter to his brother Henry: the confrontation between capital and labor in the United States (not including the Haymarket riot "which has nothing to do with knights of labor") was "a most healthy phase of evolution, a little costly, but normal, and sure to do lots of good to all hands in the end."[20] His praise for contention even pertained to the academic world. When he and Hugo Munsterberg were attacked in a scholarly paper, Munsterberg urged that they write a letter of protest. James disagreed, saying: "Since those temperamental antipathies exist—why isn't it healthy that they should express themselves? For my part, I feel rather glad than otherwise that psychology is so live a subject that the psychologists should 'go for' each other in this way. . . . We ought to cultivate tough hides."[21]

To further elucidate what James valued in political action, it might be useful to contrast briefly his conception with those of Hannah Arendt and Max Weber.[22] All three respected, even celebrated, action; each thought of it at least partly in heroic terms. Arendt described the Greek polis as a community of citizens publicly engaged in deliberation, speech, and deeds. For Arendt, action reveals the nature of the self and its potentials, which is one reason why speech is crucial to it. James did not invoke the polis or even the New England town meeting, but he shared with Arendt the belief that individuals develop their potentialities through self-sacrifice for the common good.[23] Action, in other words, is a way to combine the development and expression of the highest human capacities with the welfare of the community.

Like Arendt (and Tocqueville), James did not trust power located in large institutions, including the nation-state, and concluded that the way to resist oppressive institutional power was for individuals and groups to act.[24] In an oft-cited passage, James announced:

> I am against bigness and greatness in all their forms. . . . The bigger the unit you deal with, the hollower, the more brutal, the more mendacious is the life displayed. So I am against all big organizations as such, national ones first and foremost; against all big successes and big results; and in favor of the eternal forces of truth which always work in the individual . . . under-dogs always, till history comes, after they are long dead, and puts them on the top.[25]

He declared that the political deterioration of America in the second half of the nineteenth century was "the direct outcome of the added power of government, the corruptions and inflations of the war. . . . Every war leaves such miserable legacies, fatal seeds of future war and revolution, unless the civic virtues of the people save the State in time." This condition of political degradation, brought on by a bloated post–Civil War state and by the war itself, could be cured only by "the civic virtues of the people." He continued:

> Democracy is still upon its trial. The civic genius of our people is its only bulwark, and neither laws nor monuments, neither battleships nor public libraries, nor great newspapers nor booming stocks; neither me-

chanical invention nor political adroitness, nor churches nor universities nor civil-service examinations can save us from degeneration if the inner mystery be lost.[26]

The greatest threat to the democratic spirit is overwhelming institutions. James criticized "civilization, with its herding and branding, licensing and degree-giving, authorizing and appointing, and in general regulating and administering by system the lives of human beings."[27]

Like James, in "Politics as a Vocation" Max Weber tried to establish the place of creative action in a world in which bureaucracies are the characteristic political form. According to Weber, instead of thinking imaginatively, each person in a bureaucratic organization must carry out the orders of the person or committee above. Expertly trained administrators set the limits on action, and creative thought becomes a threat to established procedures. Because political knowledge comes to be identified as rules, regulations, procedures, and budgets, the archetypal political leader becomes the lawyer, i.e., the one who can master the rules of law, while political knowledge based on experience and custom is denigrated. James could have endorsed Weber's description of the ideal politician who serves as an alternative to the bureaucrat. Weber defined politics as *"independent leadership in action,"* saying that the politician must have three qualities: a feeling of responsibility; passion, i.e., devotion to a cause rather than excessive feeling or romanticism; and a sense of proportion, distance from things and men that allows control of the passions.[28] The desire to preserve passion, responsibility, and proportion—three characteristics of an effective and a humane political actor—was shared by Weber and James. James's fear of such institutions, and his desire to increase the space for public action, was shared by Tocqueville, Weber, and Arendt.

## II

R. B. Perry claimed that James's contribution to social and political thought is the "exaltation of direct action, and hence of both revolution and of dictatorship."[29] James believed that in order to have "depth," people "must multiply their [ideals'] sentimental surface by the dimension of the active will."[30] In other words, people should not just hold ideals but act upon them.[31] One phrase he used for healthy existence is "the strenuous life," which Browning asserted is James's "normative vision of the human." The strenuous mood leads people to confront life's difficulties whereas the easygoing mood seeks to escape them and accept present conditions.[32]

The use of the term "strenuous life" reveals a powerful tension in James between a democratic appreciation for the quotidian efforts of ordinary citizens and an elitist appeal for heroes, geniuses, and saints to embody the strenuous life, allowing the rest of us, who are less vigorous, to follow. Sometimes his call for acting upon ideals is addressed to all citizens and at other times to the few. I will present the evidence for this tension in James by continuing to compare his views on action with those of Arendt and then with the views of social Darwinists Herbert Spencer and Grant Allen. Before addressing the theme of individualism, I will try to make some sense of the tension by suggesting that James embodies the conflict between liberalism and democracy on the issue of political action.

James's own life exemplified both the heroic and the ordinary models of action that he advocated. In his efforts to provide leadership, he joined committees for public causes; wrote open letters about education, imperialism, and lynching; and directly participated in protests against U.S. involvement in the Philippines. He endorsed Jane Addams's settlement house projects, and she cited him in her autobiography as an inspiration for Hull-House. As a philosopher, he endeavored to instruct and lead the nation.[33] Not only did he teach at a prominent university, but he attempted to reach broader audiences through public lectures that formed the basis for most of his books. In these lectures, James did not exclusively address the elite. His appeal to posit and fulfill their ideals went out to everyone: working people and the wealthy, educated and uneducated.

In addition to broadly defining his audience, James expressed his democratic intention in his immediate, vivacious writing to reach that audience, writing that was in marked contrast to the prose of most textbooks and philosophical treatises. He maintained that academics needed to change their style of communication with the public if they were going to shape the democratic temperament, and he made this point explicit in a lecture directed specifically at college students and faculty. Whereas many people see in the university "a kind of sterilized conceit and incapacity for being pleased," colleges need to become more engaging because "if a college, through the inferior human influences that have grown regnant there, fails to catch the robuster tone, its failure is colossal, for its social function stops: democracy gives it a wide berth, turns toward it a deaf ear."[34] James did not think that intellectuals should rule the nation, but he did believe they have a specific contribution to make to a democracy (a point I elaborate upon in Chapter 5). If they do not connect with their audience, they cannot make that contribution.

James championed two types of action as a way to express creative energy, to reduce the possibility of violence, to preserve and improve America's representative system of government, and to contribute to the common good. The first type of action might today be called "public service" in politics, medicine, education, the arts, technological invention and manual labor that serve public needs, and social work; in fact, James praised any activity that helps others. He even thought that most people are heroic in the sense of meeting the challenges of everyday life. The second type of action is more heroic, unusual, or unique. He recognized that the values and institutions of societies are periodically transformed and posited that these transformations are led by visionaries or geniuses who are able to envision alternative social arrangements and draw people to support them in making change. This type of action is close to what Arendt meant by beginning something new.[35]

In defining a public contribution, James was highly democratic. He did not sharply distinguish the public from the private sphere, as Arendt was to do.[36] Whereas Arendt located action in the public realm, James saw the achievement of a personal goal, such as giving up drinking, as a form of action. James said, "To keep out of the gutter is for us here no part of consciousness at all, yet for many of our brethren it is the most legitimately engrossing of ideals."[37] Historian George Fredrickson says that James defined action as belief and "internal effort," but that formulation is correct only if one remembers how important it was to James that people strive to realize their visions.[38] It is not enough, he said, merely to hold an ideal; one must act on it. "Mere ideals are the cheapest things in life. . . . The more ideals a man has, the more contemptible, on the whole, do you continue to deem him, if the matter ends there for him, and if none of the laboring man's virtues are called into action on his part—no courage shown, no privations undergone, no dirt or scars contracted in the attempt to get them realized."[39] In general, a good, worthwhile, or, to use James's word, "significant" life means striving to fulfill an ideal that will contribute to the public good.[40] His formula seemed to be, "from each according to his ability."

> Individuals can add to the welfare of the [human] race in a variety of ways. You may delight its senses or "taste" by some production of luxury or art, comfort it by discovering some moral truth, relieve its pain by concocting a new patent medicine, save its labor by a bit of machinery, or by some application of a natural product. You may open a road, help start some social or business institution, contribute your mite in *any* way to the mass of the work which each generation subtracts from the task of the next; and you will come into *real* relations with your brothers—with some of them at least.[41]

The democratic character of James's description of action is plain. These actions have to do with everyday life; they are demanding, but not heroic in the sense that either Arendt or James himself sometimes demanded.

James deconstructed elitism in his essay "What Makes a Life Significant," beginning with the proposition that "morally exceptional individuals . . . worked and endured in obedience to some inner *ideal,* whilst their comrades were not actuated by anything worthy of that name." The narrowness and elitism of this formulation are then decimated. His definition of ideals expands to include self-challenge, the effort "to enlarge . . . sympathetic insight into fellow-lives," learning to love and forgive others through religion, voluntary labor, voluntary poverty, and "class-loyalty." Although at first appearing blind to the ideals of others, James then made the possibility of blindness an explicit theme, identifying as an important ideal the overcoming of blindness to the struggles, achievements, and inner meaning of others' lives.

> The barrenness and ignobleness of the more usual laborer's life consist in the fact that it is moved by no such inner springs. The backache, the long hours, the danger, are patiently endured—for what? To gain a quid of tobacco, a glass of beer, a cup of coffee, a meal, a bed, and to begin again the next day and shirk as much as one can. [This is why soldiers are honored, not laborers. But] the plot now thickens. . . . We have seen the blindness and deadness to each other which are our

natural inheritance; and in spite of them, we have been led to acknowledge an inner meaning which passeth show, and which may be present in the lives of others where we least descry it.[42]

Significant action has been redefined as the struggle to fulfill an ideal, to overcome the difficulties put in one's way, and to appreciate the ideals and struggles of others.

## III

James not only espoused action but portrayed to his readers a world in which action is meaningful. Individuals can collectively alter the currents of history, at least to some degree, according to their plans and ideals. "What are the causes that make communities change from generation to generation?" he asked in *Will to Believe*, answering that citizens and their leaders make change; history is not determined by God, evolution, technology, or the economy.[43]

The scientific theories of Charles Darwin powerfully influenced American thought after the Civil War and were taken to have a variety of political implications. James indicted the social Darwinism of Spencer and Allen as a philosophical buttress of resignation because it implied, in the authoritative language of science, that individuals cannot deliberately shape history.[44] Most details of the debate between James and these social Darwinists are not worth recounting because that specific version of social Darwinism is no longer current. Today, determinism takes different forms as many people continue to believe that change cannot be made thoughtfully and creatively.[45] Therefore, I describe only enough of the social Darwinist position, as described by one of its critics, to get a flavor of it in order to elucidate James's models of political action.

According to intellectual historian Richard Hofstadter, James endeavored "to redeem spontaneity and indeterminacy from the oppressive causal network of Spencerian social evolution."[46] In several essays, James indicted Spencer and Allen for believing that social change was not created by human beings. "Mr. Spencer . . . and his disciple, Mr. Grant Allen . . . hold that no individual initiative has any effect in determining the course of human destiny."[47] Allen said that great leaders are produced by their countries, not by accident; the masses of citizens are more important than the great individual; it is the common characteristics of a particular people that are crucial, not the exceptional personalities; history creates important figures while leaders do not create history and barely affect it; leaders are available when needed and are replaceable, i.e., history occurs without the conscious choice of individuals. Finally, Allen and Spencer saw the mind as passive, merely reflecting the environment.[48]

> The Spencerian school [believed that historical] changes are irrespective of persons and independent of individual control. They are due to the environment, to the circumstances . . . the increasing experience of outer relations; to everything, in fact, except the Grants and the Bismarcks, the Joneses and the Smiths. . . . [Determinism] professes that those parts of the universe already laid down absolutely appoint and decree what the other parts shall be.[49]

Even though at the end of nineteenth century the Knights of Labor, the Populists, anarchists, suffragettes, and African-American activists tried to overcome determinism in practice, James refuted it at the level of theory by emphasizing the importance of individual initiatives.

James's conception of science as applied to politics was different from that of the social Darwinists. Underlying the conflict over science was a dispute over the possibilities of political action. Believing that change resulted from large social forces, the Darwinists sought to develop a social science to map the direction of mass behavior whereas James's model of science and social change was more experimental: visionaries proffered new paths for society, and with the people's support, those paths might be successfully walked. Obviously, far more paths were advocated than taken.

James called his outlook "meliorism" in contrast to pessimism and optimism. He described the pessimist as one who believes that the salvation of the world is impossible whereas the optimist thinks it inevitable. Since readers today might not call social change "salvation," one could substitute such terms as "justice," "equality," or "democracy." Between pessimism and optimism, James posited, stands "meliorism," which means that salvation is possible but not guaranteed. What is the meliorist model of change?

Take, for example, any one of us in this room with the ideals which he cherishes, and is willing to live and work for. Every such ideal realized will be one moment in the world's salvation. But these particular ideals are not bare abstract possibilities. They are grounded, they are *live* possibilities, for we are their live champions and pledges, and if the complementary conditions come and add themselves, our ideals will become actual things. . . . [The conditions are something not predetermined but] a chance, a gap that we can spring into, and, finally, *our act.*

Does our act then *create* the world's salvation so far as it makes room for itself, so far as it leaps into the gap? Does it create, not the whole world's salvation of course, but just so much of this as itself covers of the world's extent?[50]

By the last sentence, James implied that change will not be universal, interconnected. He imagined that a critic will respond, "Irrational! . . . How can new being come in local spots and patches which add themselves or stay away at random, independently of the rest?" James replied: "The only *real* reason I can think of why anything should ever come is that *someone wishes it to be here.* It is *demanded,* demanded, it may be, to give relief to no matter how small a fraction of the world's mass. This is the *living reason,* and compared with it material causes and logical necessities are spectral things." Creating change requires that "each several agent does its own 'level best.'" The implication of this model of change is that the world becomes open to possibilities both of greatness and of horror. The world is a "real adventure, with real danger . . . a social scheme of co-operative work genuinely to be done."[51]

As an alternative to the social Darwinists, who minimized agency in shaping history, James's two models of change are both based on combining ideals and action. Sometimes James stressed the leadership of an elite that would, with the support of the people, reshape politics, society, and culture according to new ideals. A variant model of change adhered to the boundaries on action set by the Constitution; accepting national institutions, James called on ordinary people to preserve popular government by their active, informed participation in a government whose principles they understand and embrace.

James is at his most elitist in his essay "Great Men and Their Environment," in which he advanced an alternative interpretation to that of Spencer and Allen of the implications of Darwin's evolutionary theory for political change. Darwin identified two central factors in the process of evolution: free variation, i.e., the new capacities of a species brought about by mutation, and natural selection, which maintains or destroys the variations. James compared natural selection with the historical factors that affect the success or failure of individual initiatives. Without discounting the importance of historical context for political action, James took free variation to be the more important factor in social change. The mind of the "genius" or "great man" is like Darwin's spontaneous variation. Such minds do not reproduce existing ideas, customs, and institutions; they develop new visions, values, and laws—not unlike Nietzsche's supermen.[52] Not all geniuses are successful; many are so out of sync with their times and the popular mood that they are ignored. And most people living in stable conditions accept the ideas and institutions under which they live and are not open to revolutionary leadership.[53] But other leaders do gain the support of the people, and these are the founders of new parties and nations, religions and institutions, movements and organizations. History evolves, said James, by the popular support of great leaders' initiatives.

In *Will to Believe*, James wrote in a Nietzschean vein, saying that existing conditions, unbearably soft and dull, must be overcome by great leaders. In other moods, James's notion of change is more modest and respectful of what exists. Both strains of thought can be seen clearly in "What Makes a Life Significant." He there relates a visit to an assembly, something like a summer school for the wealthy intelligentsia, at Chautauqua in upstate New York:

> Sobriety and industry, intelligence and goodness, orderliness and ideality, prosperity and cheerfulness, pervade the air. . . . You have the best of company, and yet no effort. You have no zymotic diseases, no poverty, no drunkenness, no crime, no police. . . . You have, in short,

a foretaste of what human society might be, were it all in the light, with no suffering and no dark corners. . . . And yet what was my own astonishment, on emerging into the dark and wicked world again, to catch myself quite unexpectedly and involuntarily saying: "Ouf! what a relief! Now for something primordial and savage, even though it were as bad as an Armenian massacre, to set the balance straight again. This order is too tame, this culture too second-rate, this goodness too uninspiring."[54]

I quote this passage as an accurate description of a certain Jamesian mood, but his final judgment on Chautauqua is different: "Grant that at Chautauqua there was little moral effort, little sweat or muscular strain in view. Still, deep down in the souls of the participants we may be sure that something of the sort was hid, some inner stress, some vital virtue not found wanting when required."[55] In this democratic humor, James realized that when we tend to think any group is worth writing off we are probably wrong.

James recognized and criticized his aristocratic moments as "ancestral blindness," but he did have them. With uncharacteristic harshness, James spoke of "human intelligences of a simple order" that are literal, governed by habit, and take things for granted. Their "faithfulness and honesty" is "the single gift by which they are sometimes able to warm us into admiration. . . . [But this simple intelligence is really more like] a piece of inanimate matter than . . . the steadfastness of a human will capable of alternative choice." James also referred to "the herd of nullities whose votes count for zero in the march of events," and he contrasted this "herd" with "examples and leaders of opinion or potentates, and in general those to whose actions, position or genius gives a far-reaching human import" and with a third group, "the rest of us."[56] James may have harshly criticized the masses, not only because of ancestral class prejudice, but as an overreaction to the social Darwinist dismissal of individual effort and their claim that aggregates of human beings are the sole historical force. Or he could have been influenced by Emerson's essay "Representative Men," by Thomas Carlyle's *On Heroes and Hero-Worship,* or by Nietzsche himself.[57]

Even while acknowledging the aristocratic cruelty of his words, one might hope to rescue James as a democrat by saying that his views represent an early position. Both Coon and Cotkin write of James's radicalization in the 1890s, but in James's essay "The Social Value of the College-Bred," written in 1907 just three years before his death, a similar elitist model of change appears, albeit with less vituperation.[58]

> The notion that a people can run itself and its affairs anonymously is now well known to be the silliest of absurdities. Mankind does nothing save through initiatives on the part of inventors, great or small, and imitation by the rest of us—these are the sole factors active in human progress. Individuals of genius show the way, and set the patterns, which common people then adopt and follow. . . . In our democracy, where everything else is so shifting, we alumni and alumnae of the colleges are the only permanent presence that corresponds to the aristocracy in older countries.

James contended that colleges should teach "the sense for human superiority." Confusingly, James claimed that the purpose of accepting "superiority" is to save democracy from those who would reject it on the grounds that the people inevitably choose inferior leaders and spurn "higher" human qualities. Without good leaders, democracy "may undergo self-poisoning." This line of thought did not induce James to echo Henry and Brooks Adams in their rejection of democracy; James called democracy "a kind of religion, and we are bound not to admit its failure."[59]

In summary, James's emphasis on great men and his moments of contempt for the many are certainly elitist, but his second model of political action, in which average citizens are active, is consonant with democracy. James seems torn between democratic and elitist sentiments. At his most snobbish he saw geniuses and leaders as the only people who matter in history. Educated leaders and great individuals guide the "ordinary" people, who need only recognize, respect, and follow these qualified leaders. At other times he implied that the average person can make a more active contribution to public life. He indicated that representative government requires vigilance and participation on the part of the people, and he discerned in everyone, no matter what their social position, the capacity for free action and the possession of ideas and positions that must be recognized in making political decisions.

# IV

James's democratic side was revealed in an 1897 speech at the unveiling of a statue of Robert Gould Shaw when James urged Americans to learn patriotic self-sacrifice from Shaw: "In such an emergency Americans of all complexions and conditions can go forth like brothers, and meet death cheerfully if need be, in order that this religion of our native land shall not become a failure on the earth."[60] In seeming contradiction to some of his comments in "The Social Value of the College-Bred," James again called democracy America's religion and defined it as self-rule by the citizens. "Our nation had been founded in what we may call our American religion, baptized and reared in the faith that a man requires no master to take care of him, and that common people can work out their salvation well enough together if left free to try." Here a condition of political health is depicted as citizens' attending to politics, choosing their leaders wisely, and acting generously toward one another. Not only leaders but citizens must act. Because people possess an instinct for war, Shaw's extraordinary bravery in battle need not be emulated as much as his "lonely courage (civic courage as we call it in peace-times)." Civic courage enabled Shaw to lead an African-American regiment in the face of calumny by many fellow soldiers and citizens. This form of courage is admirable, but not epic; to put it another way, heroic impulses must be channeled into seemingly modest activities.

> The nation blest above all nations is she in whom the civic genius of the people does the saving day by day, by acts without external picturesqueness; by speaking, writing, voting reasonably; by smiting corruption swiftly; by good temper between parties; by the people knowing true men when they see them, and preferring them as leaders to rabid partisans or empty quacks.[61]

It is difficult to know how to assess James's politics here. Does he ask for anything more than loyalty to the state? A generous reading of James's image of popular activity may concede that he did not envision the Paris Commune but called for something closer to radical democracy than our present condition of widespread disillusioned withdrawal from public life.

His vision of civic courage may seem inadequate, but it is not negligible if one thinks of the alternative: popular support for extremists such as George Wallace, Ross Perot, David Duke, and Russian nationalist Vladimir Zhirinovsky. Not demanding that most people accomplish extraordinary deeds may even be a form of political respect. Although everyone has civic duties to perform, which are necessary for the health of the country and community, we should not hate ourselves if we are not activists.[62] There is heroism, James declared, in just getting on with our lives: fulfilling our obligations while confronting the setbacks, losses, and pain inherent in existence.[63] James's Darwinian model of politics is democratic in that it calls on everyone to participate and recognizes that the few geniuses cannot alter history solely by their own wills and activities. The tension between James's political models might be further illuminated if they are compared to the civil rights and feminist movements, two of the most important radical democratic mass campaigns of recent times.

V

James's theory of leadership seems to be one of his most undemocratic stances, but the matter is more complicated than it at first appears. In comparing his theory of leadership to ideas articulated by the theorists of recent democratic movements, I am not suggesting that James is in a one-to-one relationship with, or a direct antecedent of, these theorists; instead, I suggest that some of the positions they articulate concerning leadership resonate with propositions of James while others go beyond him. For example, James said that one leader is insufficient to initiate change: "Sporadic great men come everywhere. But for a community to get vibrating through and through with intensely active life, many geniuses coming together and in rapid succession are required. This is why great epochs are so rare."[64] This image seems to fit the civil rights movement in which numerous leaders have emerged, including Dr. Martin Luther King, Jr., James Bevel, Andrew Young, Stokely Carmichael, Diane Nash, Rosa Parks, Fannie Lou Hamer, Robert Moses, Ella Baker, Jesse Jackson, and James Farmer. To suggest that such leaders, whom I see as examples of James's "geniuses," have played essential roles in the movement is not an inherently elitist proposition.

Even the most egalitarian theorists of change acknowledge a role for authorities within a movement, if only as teachers. Democratic activists Ella Baker, Robert Moses, and Starhawk might accept James's assertion that change is sparked by individuals who possess creative vision and conceive of strategies for achieving their visions, but they would not see, as James sometimes did, a large gulf in talent between the leaders and the many. Civil rights organizer Baker conceded the need for visionaries when she said:

> From a practical standpoint, anyone who looked at the Harlem area knew that the potential for integration *per se* was basically impossible unless there were some radically innovative things done. And those innovative things would not be acceptable to those who ran the school system, nor to communities, nor even to the people who call themselves supporters of integration.[65]

In this situation, leadership is necessary to see the possibility of change, to create a plan to achieve it, and to move in an unfamiliar direction. Baker differed from James in seeing the group as the innovators, not individuals. Furthermore, she rejected the tendency within the civil rights movement to identify leaders as the primary agents of change. "I have always thought," she said, "what is needed is the development of people who are interested not in being leaders as much as in developing leadership among other people."[66] Feminist theorist Starhawk is closer to James when she acknowledges the need for leadership in asserting: "A group . . . needs a brain. It needs some people who are willing to look ahead, anticipate problems, suggest new directions, try out new solutions, keep track of information and decisions, who lead in the sense of stepping out in front and going first. Such leadership is a service to the group."[67] The danger, she says, comes from hidden leaders, unaccountable to the others who use power for self-interest.

To claim that there are no leaders, as radical democrats have at times claimed, does not eliminate them or their legitimate function. The leader is in essence a teacher, and James had faith that leaders will bring out the creative potential of average citizens. He proclaimed, "In picking out from history our heroes, and communing with their kindred spirits . . . each one of us may best fortify and inspire what creative energy may be in his own soul."[68] He thought that heroes, geniuses, and saints inspire creativity on the part of the many rather than squelch it.[69] To the same end, civil rights organizer Robert Moses wanted to identify and develop local leadership and create mass participation.[70] Although he "recognized how easily the creative potential of people can be crushed by leaders and institutions," Moses did not dismiss their necessity. He insisted that once a movement is started, if people are allowed to develop they will become leaders. Like Moses, James feared the stultifying effect of institutions on the citizenry, and both James and Moses believed that leaders would develop spontaneously. James called the process "free variation" while Moses said: "Leadership is there in the people. . . . You don't have to worry about that. You don't have to worry about where your leaders are, how are we going to get some leaders. The leadership is there. If you go out and work with your people, then the leadership will emerge. . . . We don't know who they are now; we don't need to know. But the leadership will emerge from the movement that emerges."[71] Inspiration is precisely the effect that James, Baker, Starhawk, and Moses want leaders to have, although the contemporary activists see more clearly than did James the danger that leaders might substitute their initiatives for those of the people and thereby foster either passivity or blind obedience.

# VI

The tension between James's elitist and democratic tendencies has gone largely unremarked by commentators, but he has frequently been called an "individualist," a word that covers a multitude of sins, including political impotence, lack of interest in politics, naive idealism, relativism, and an underestimation of the importance of institutions.[72] According to political theorist Richard Flathman, James, despite his intentions, "promoted an individuality so radical that it threatened solipsism and even denial of the desirability of mutual intelligibility."[73] Cornel West describes James as "a libertarian, with circumscribed democratic sentiments, an international outlook, and deep moral sensitivity. This perspective is one of political impotence, yet it buttresses moral integrity and promotes the exercise of individual conscience."[74]

"Unlike Dewey, his successor in the pragmatic tradition," wrote historian Richard Hofstadter, "James was guilty of only the remotest interest in systematic or collective social reform. One expression of his fundamental individualism is the fact that . . . he had no sustained interest in social theory as such. He always dealt with philosophical problems in individual terms."[75] Santayana criticized his former teacher for believing that people could shape events according to their ideals.[76] According to Santayana, James

> held a false moralistic view of history, attributing events to the conscious motives and free will of individuals; whereas individuals, especially in governments, are creatures of circumstance and slaves to vested interests. These interests may be more or less noble, romantic, or sordid, but they inevitably entangle and subjugate men of action.[77]

Political scientist Gary Jacobsohn writes that pragmatism promotes individualism by encouraging each person to make up his or her own mind about the truth, and George Fredrickson argues that James's anti-institutionalism opposed the spirit of his time which called for larger, more active government.[78] Even James called himself an individualist: "We 'intellectuals' in America must all work to keep our precious birthright of individualism, and freedom from these institutions. *Every* great institution is perforce a means of corruption—whatever good it may also do. Only in the free personal relation is full ideality to be found."[79] Elsewhere he said, "The practical consequence of [pluralism] is the well-known democratic respect for the sacredness of individuality."[80]

This formulation indicates that James linked democracy with individualism, and I would argue that James's conception of individualism is compatible with democracy but that he used the term "individualism" in a way that might be misleading to political theorists. James's conception of individualism is not necessarily corrosive of politics or community, and his understanding of that term was quite different from that of Tocqueville in *Democracy in America*, in which Tocqueville said: "Individualism is a calm and considered feeling which disposes each citizen to isolate himself from the mass of his fellows and withdraw into the circle of family and friends; with this little society formed to his taste, he gladly leaves the greater society to look after itself."[81] James's individuals are not at all isolated: they have powerful obligations to their society, including that of becoming active and alert citizens. Our common duty is to improve the world.[82] James insisted in "The Moral Equivalent of War," "All the qualities of a man acquire dignity when he knows that the service of the collectivity that owns him needs them."[83] At the age of twenty-six, James pronounced:

> Our predecessors, even apart from the physical link of generation, have made us what we are. Every thought you now have and every act and intention owes its complexion to the acts of your dead and living brothers. *Everything* we know and are is through men. . . . [A] sympathy with men as such, and a desire to contribute to the weal of a species, which . . . contains All that we acknowledge as good, may very well form an external interest sufficient to keep one's moral pot boiling in a very lively manner to a good old age.[84]

James saw citizens as being connected by ties of friendship, tradition, and shared ideals, and judging by his comments on the philosophy of Thomas Davidson, individualism meant to James something like independence, originality, and eccentricity.[85]

The question is not, Was James an individualist? but, rather, What did he mean by individualism and did it undermine his democratic commitments? He did not uphold private rights against the public good, although he thought the individual should be protected from a large, invasive state. If he believed that the individual is in some sense "sacred," he also assumed that each person has ties and obligations to others. This ambiguity is reflected, but not noted, in commentaries on James, even though commentators who label him an individualist also note strong communitarian elements in his thinking. "Overall he made good his claim that one who upholds an ethic of democratic individualism is obligated to take part in social or political change," stated Gerald Myers. Hofstadter conceded that James "in his later years . . . viewed the rise of collectivism with satisfaction and found a means of reconciling it with his characteristic emphasis on individual activity." McDermott explained that "for James, it is precisely the ability of man to enter into the relational fabric of the world, in a participative and liberating way, which enables him to become human."[86]

For James, individualism is compatible with socialism. By socialism, James surely did not mean state-owned property or means of production but something like democracy, justice, community, and equality. Although Davidson rejected the label "socialist," "no one felt more deeply than he the evils of rapacious individual competition. . . . Spontaneously and flexibly organized social settlements or communities, with individual leaders as their centers seem to have been his ideal, each with its own religious or ethical elements of discipline."[87] In "The Moral Equivalent of War," James embraced a vaguely defined socialism: "I will now confess my own utopia. I devoutly believe in the ultimate reign of peace and in the gradual advent of some sort of a socialistic equilibrium."[88]

James's democratic socialist individualism seems to be another instance in which he confounds the categories employed to understand him. What type of individualist calls for socialism? How could he reconcile these seemingly opposite values? The answer might lie in what James intended by the terms. Although James used the word "individualism," he consistently separated individualism from self-interest. James's individualism was quite close to communitarian anarchism and the doctrine that each individual should make a unique contribution to the common good, and that each should be allowed to define that contribution in his or her own way. James was an individualist who did not put economic freedom or personal rights ahead of the common good. He did not see public obligations or communal hegemony as dangerous to individuals, but, in the spirit of Tocqueville's fear of "democratic despotism," James dreaded a powerful state that leaves no place for eccentricity or human initiatives on behalf of the community. His view of the potential contribution of each individual to the common good may be utopian, but his utopia is democratic.[89]

I have shown that James advanced two models of action: the first challenges people to make that contribution to the public good of which they were capable; the second is revolutionary and creates a new body politic, described as founding, by Machiavelli in *The Prince*. Examples of such founders include Moses, George Washington, and Lenin. What is the relationship between the two models of action? James did not make it clear. The heroic is extraordinary, and he hoped that citizens will become more public spirited in everyday life before institutions are radically transformed. He explicitly asserted in "The Moral Equivalent of War" that the impulse to do great deeds for the common good is healthy but needs to be transmuted from war to public service. He was not afraid of direct action, such as strikes, but opposed violence and the denigration of one's opponents.

James believed that American institutions would be strengthened if the citizenry embraced as civic duties attending carefully to politics, debating issues publicly, and choosing their leaders carefully. He did not seem to realize, however, that the American institutions and liberal political values he embraced fostered the centralization, selfishness, and passivity that he deplored.[90] He did not appear to grasp, as Rousseau did in *The Social Contract*, that representation can be taken as a substitute for direct action. James's celebration of action may have been democratic, but his liberalism undermined that contribution. There may be a component of privatism in James's individualism that undermined the realization of his desire for people to make a contribution to the public good and to adopt the obligations to others required by political participation. Nevertheless, James stretched the confines of liberalism; the liberal elements of his thought strive with the radical democratic elements. And even James's liberalism is worthy of respect. One comes away from reading James reflecting that if his advice to the American body politic were heeded, citizens would be more active than they are today and less inclined to define a full human life as one devoted to the accumulation of luxuries by working and trading for profit while enjoying the pleasures of private life.

## Chapter 2
# *James and Gender*

For a pacifist and socialist, James found a lot to praise in war and warriors. He believed war brought out virtues that could be tapped for the public good and advocated sublimating the aggressive instinct into public service. Admittedly, James's model of politics resembles the one criticized by feminist theorists as he invited his fellow citizens to be "manly."

> A life is manly, stoical, moral, or philosophical, we say, in proportion as it is less swayed by paltry personal considerations and more by objective ends that call for energy, even though that energy bring personal loss and pain. This is the good side of war, in so far as it calls for "volunteers." And for morality life is a war, and the service of the highest is a sort of cosmic patriotism which also calls for volunteers.[1]

> We must make new energies and hardihoods continue the manliness to which the military mind so faithfully clings. Martial virtues must be the enduring cement; intrepidity, contempt of softness, surrender of private interest, obedience to command, must still remain the rock upon which states are built.[2]

Obviously, James's language here is gender-laden as he calls on his fellow-citizens to adopt "manliness" rather than effeminacy. Women have often been associated with nature, so James's call for "an army enlisted against *nature*" in "The Moral Equivalent of War" has an ominous ring.[3] One feminist critic of James indicts him: "In a nation in which one out of four women can expect to be raped in her lifetime, a child is sexually abused every two minutes, and wife beating is rampant, it is downright immoral to join [James] in his praise of the rack of contempt of softness."[4]

Understanding that feminist theory is not monolithic, in this chapter I look at aspects of James's theory of action that might be ignored had

33

feminist theorists not made them prominent—specifically, his gender-based language and his ideas about women, war, human nature, and asceticism.[5] My central question is the effect of such language on James's conception of action. Does the fact that he desired people to behave "manfully" indicate that his models of action were misogynist, instigated violence, or subverted his professed commitment to the common good? I do not dismiss the possibility that they were and did, and do not intend to say that James was only employing the vocabulary current in his day. I will argue, however, that except when it came to the family, James so mixed gender stereotypes, and had so much goodwill toward women who broke through the Victorian constrictions on them, that his language is, for the most part, not harmful. It is outmoded and unnecessary, and he excessively employed military metaphors for public service, but James was in most ways a liberal feminist and came close to postmodern feminism by confounding the gender categories of his age. James's military vocabulary is easily misinterpreted. Although he invoked heroism, sacrifice, and battlefields, his goal was to claim that language for everyday nonviolent contributions to the common good, a claim that places his work much closer to the values held by some feminist theorists than his vocabulary might lead us to believe.

I write here with two audiences in mind, both of which I count as friends: one is composed of feminists who are skeptical of James, especially when they hear how he discusses action and women. I want to persuade them that James was not only an ally but a useful one. The other audience thinks that some feminist scholarship makes too much fuss about language and that vocabulary should be set aside in order to get to the real issues. In James's case these people are partly right, but a study of his vocabulary nonetheless raises substantive questions.

In purporting to depict a "feminist" theory of political action and its associated critique of the masculine ideal, I fear that my subject has vanished or at least metamorphosed. In the 1960s and 1970s, as women were fighting to enter both mainstream and alternative politics, the issue of whether or not to play the political game according to rules written by men was quite lively. Today, despite the persistence of the glass ceiling, which blocks women from occupying top positions in government and industry, women have entered political life, and new, often quite subtle, theoretical concerns have emerged.[6] Nevertheless, my primary concentration is on political action, and therefore the previous wave of feminist theory, which was preoccupied with the nature of action, remains of great interest to me. I contend that James supported an expanded role for women similar to the one called for by feminists since Charlotte Brontë and that he broke down gender definitions in a way reminiscent of postmodern feminists. There remain, however, elements of James's conception of women that are essentialist and reactionary.

# I

It might be asked, What is so terrible about masculine politics? According to some feminist theorists, masculine politics was defined by the ancient Greeks and by later theorists such as Machiavelli, Hobbes, and Hannah Arendt. Wendy Brown lists as "manly" political values: "devotion to personal power, heroism, violence, domination and 'the extraordinary,' antipathy to everyday existence, and the instrumental rationality with which all of these things are infused."[7] Christine Di Stefano sees masculine ideology as a "combative brand of dualistic thinking," one that strives for a secure, fixed identity, radical individualism, and fear of and hostility toward anything feminine.[8] In her view, masculine politics relies excessively on self-discipline and conquering one's emotions—or at least suppressing fear, pity, and compassion while expressing rage and competitiveness.[9]

Masculine politics is also criticized for being abstract. In the masculine ideal, men sacrifice their lives for valor or to uphold a principle whereas the actions and sacrifices of women are tied to other people; typically, they would die not for "the cause," but they would die for friends, lovers, and family.[10] One reason for the abstract nature of masculine politics is that male theorists since the ancient Greeks have sharply distinguished public from private life.[11] The Greeks excluded women from participation in politics and separated the domain of the household from the public realm. To be confined to the home, as women and slaves were, was to be chained to necessity, to activities required for mere life; in contrast, the political arena was the site of freedom. Politics became abstract by turning its back on the common, private, and everyday.

Once women are excluded, political life reflects an aggressive masculine personality. Another explanation of this personality is provided by the psychoanalytic theory of object-relations. Men become pugnacious in order to attain their autonomy: to become men they must distinguish and separate themselves from women, beginning with their mothers.[12] "The principle of masculinity," Di Stefano writes, "rests on the repression of what is deemed feminine."[13] Women, on the other hand, develop by imitating their mothers and therefore have connection rather than distance at the heart of their identity formation.[14]

Whether masculine politics originates in child development, ideology, the split between public and private, or ancient customs, its greatest dangers include war and the suppression of women's potentialities, which is a type of violence.[15] Peace is rejected as being feminine and therefore contemptuous.[16] The citizen is modeled on the warrior, but a participatory democracy composed of citizen warriors may self-destruct.[17] Nancy Hartsock asks: "Is the masculine political actor, the citizen warrior, capable of inhabiting a real democracy, that is, a world of equals who engage in rational consideration of the right actions for the community as a whole? Or is he more at home in agonistic and competitive settings where he can pursue the attainment of glory and honor?[18] From this critical standpoint, the warlike spirit of James's ideal citizens would eventually destroy democracy, community, and peace.[19] James has been accused of advocating action for its own sake and of praising the "will to power" while pragmatism is frequently criticized for lacking a test or standard by which success in action or "good consequences" can be measured. The danger is that power and efficacy become goals in themselves.

If masculine politics is to be jettisoned, what should take its place?[20] Some feminist theorists have posited that women—through biology, psychology, experience, or tradition—bring different values and viewpoints to public life.[21] If men have sought to prove their masculinity with guns and brawls, resulting in a politics of competition and violence, women have not relied on physical force to accomplish their ends.[22] And although they have been frequently controlled, women have not always lacked influence. They therefore can teach men how to achieve power without autonomy and domination.

Other conceptions of feminist politics separate it from actual women. Feminist politics need not be practiced exclusively by and for women, just as masculine politics has not been practiced only by men or by all men.

Martin Luther King, Jr., because of his advocacy of nonviolence and community, may be considered a feminist political actor, and conversely, many women have shown great capability for playing the political game in its masculine configuration. Defining feminist politics by its values rather than its practitioners, one could start with the proposition that such politics would not sharply divide the personal from the political. Desire, relationships, and feelings would not be dismissed as trivial or impediments to valor but respected as proper topics for public discussion. Feminist politics would be concrete: citizens would not strive for efficiency, mastery, or power but for specific ends. Women's politics would thus be based upon tangible aims, connections with others, nonviolence, and relationships other than command and obedience.[23]

At this point Wolin suggests, as an expansion of the theoretical inquiry: "There remains a question of the conception of politics in feminist theory. Can politics be transformed so that the truly beneficial values it promotes—nurture, connection, nonviolence—are the only necessary and effective weapons and so that the type of characteristics James promotes can be dismissed? Different interests and ideals inevitably come into conflict, in this world and any imaginable world, without anything sinister about that conflict. And then one has to confront power, which is necessary to achieve one's ends and to confront the opposition's power. Can one participate in that system of power without developing some of the characteristics to which James points? To take part in any game—whether it's tennis, baseball, or skating—or in politics requires that one play by the rules. Some feminists might want to change the nature of the game, becoming radical in the sense of rejecting current understandings or conventions about the game's nature. But what happens to those things that feminists claim make it objectionable, such as the quest for power, heroism, and courage? Do war, violence, and class conflict disappear?"[24]

Feminist theory would put us on guard against James's vocabulary of action, as he seems to employ precisely the dangerous language of action that would lead to violence, if not war, and the dissolution of community by fostering agonistic competition. I do not accept the various elements of this proposition, however. Why would a pacifist resort to metaphors of war and armies? During the time James was writing, advocates of war were drawing on the heroic imagery of the Civil War in order to justify imperialist conquest. Teddy Roosevelt was using the language of "the strenuous life" to glorify war and denounce as sissies anyone who opposed imperialism. James felt it necessary to use the same language for radically different ends. James also assumed that heroic language tapped into popular instincts for aggression, self-sacrifice, and public service; he argued that any case for pacifism that did not speak to those instincts would fail. Nevertheless, understanding the reasons why James used the language does not resolve the issue of whether or not it has had a detrimental effect: has it produced more violence and buttressed traditional gender roles? I have no empirical evidence to answer that question, but it would certainly be unfortunate if Roosevelt's call to live "the strenuous life" through actual conquest were conflated by the public with James's call to live that life through nonviolent contributions to the public good.

## II

In order to determine if James is guilty of perpetuating the worst aspects of masculine politics as described by feminist theorists, we must examine his explicit views about women. In his writings on psychology, he attempted to distinguish male and female psyches, and he took up the theme of gender roles, inside and outside the family. Even if James espoused the value of "manliness," and along with most other men in his day linked "femininity" with weakness, he encouraged women to transgress their inherited roles; he criticized the Victorian stereotype for encouraging women to be weak and passive; and he judged that the pain of childbirth, the courage and self-sacrifice of motherhood, and the undertaking of physical challenges made women appropriately "manly."[25]

Here is one biographical clue to his outlook on women: James respected his women students, including Gertrude Stein and Mary Whiton Calkins. He argued vigorously, against the objections of Harvard president Charles W. Eliot, that Calkins should be accepted as a student in James's graduate psychology seminar. When all the male students registered in the seminar mysteriously withdrew, James taught Calkins in a seminar of one.[26]

In The Principles of Psychology James described men and women as being different in significant ways. Women are more optimistic, innocent, and intuitive; women become as angry as men but are more afraid to express their anger through fighting; empathy and parental love are stronger in women than in men.[27] All in all, James's notions about gender in that work are neither vicious nor visionary.[28]

In criticizing the repressive situation of women in Victorian America, at least the situation of women of his race and class, James showed that he did not accept the reigning stereotypes for them. Above all, he held that women had been coddled and rendered frivolous; indeed, he could have endorsed the narrator's proclamation in *Jane Eyre*:

It is in vain to say human beings ought to be satisfied with tranquility: they must have action; and they will make it if they cannot find it. Millions are condemned to a stiller doom than mine, and millions are in silent revolt against their lot. . . . Women are supposed to be very calm generally: but women feel just as men feel; they need exercise for their faculties, and a field for their efforts as much as their brothers do; they suffer from too rigid a constraint, too absolute a stagnation, precisely as men would suffer; and it is narrow-minded in their more privileged fellow-creatures to say that they ought to confine themselves to making puddings and knitting stockings, to playing on the piano and embroidering bags. It is thoughtless to condemn them, or laugh at them, if they seek to do more or learn more than custom has pronounced necessary for their sex.[29]

Although James praised "manly" action and criticized passivity as being "effeminate," he believed that women should be encouraged to be manly in the sense of being courageous, self-disciplined, and even heroic.[30] He wrote to his depressed daughter Margaret:

You have evidently been in a bad state of spirits again, and dissatisfied with your environment; and I judge that you have been still more dissatisfied with the inner state of trying to consume your own smoke, and grin and bear it. . . . I believe you have been trying to do the *manly thing* under difficult circumstances, but one learns only gradually to do the *best* thing . . . [which is to express one's unhappiness to loved ones, but in a controlled manner].[31]

Note that James points to a better way of behaving than doing the "manly thing."

Women could become admirably manly by undertaking strenuous physical labor, participating in sports and outdoor activities, and by becoming mothers.[32] Interpreting motherhood as an expression of civic virtue is a feminist tradition dating from the American Revolution,[33] and James emphasized the character transformation engendered by raising children:

> A woman will run among strangers in her nightgown if it be a question of saving her baby's life or her own. Take a self-indulgent woman's life in general. She will yield to every inhibition set by her disagreeable sensations, lie late in bed, live upon tea or bromides, keep indoors from the cold. Every difficulty finds her obedient to its "no." But make a mother of her, and what have you? Possessed by maternal excitement, she now confronts wakefulness, weariness, and toil without an instant of hesitation or a word of complaint. The inhibitive power of pain over her is extinguished wherever the baby's interests are at stake.[34]

Since James's word for civic virtue is "manliness," he paradoxically implies that women are being manly when they are being "true mothers." While traveling in Europe, James admired German peasant women and suggested that their physical exertion set a good example for American women, particularly for his tormented sister Alice.

> The sight of the women here has strengthened me more than ever in my belief that they ought to be made to do the hard labor of the community—they are far happier and better for it. I only wish I had that pampered Alice here to see these little runts of peasant women stumping about with their immense burdens on their backs. . . . Seriously there is a great deal of good in it—and the ideal German woman of poetry (see Goethe, for instance), is a working woman.[35]

James did not believe that women were incapable of possessing the "martial virtues" he admired, even if he labeled the passive life he feared as "feminine." Because James used "feminine" to designate characteristics typical of (childless) women of his era—not inherent or universal qualities of women per se—he showed that he was conscious of the distinction between stereotypes and actual women.[36] He feared that the pampered condition of Victorian upper-class women would become general throughout the United States, brought on partly by the socialist and feminist values he embraced. People flee pain and would create a government to alleviate it, but a world with no challenges would leave no room for action.[37] In such a world the inertness of the stereotypical Victorian woman would be appropriate.

James preferred that women become "manly" through taking part in public action, sports, and camping. Gerald Myers invokes as evidence of a feminist streak in James his support for Jane Addams and consumer advocate Pauline Goldmark and the fact that when hiking in the Adirondacks with a group that included Bryn Mawr students, on the day he fatally strained his heart, James complimented them for wearing knickerbockers. Edith Franklin Wyatt wrote: "I remember especially that he made us all feel in the van of progress . . . by saying of the convenience of our clothes for climbing—'I'm glad it's come. I'm glad I've lived to see it'—and how grateful to him I was."[38]

In an 1869 book review of John Stuart Mill's *The Subjection of Women* and Horace Bushnell's antifeminist tract, *Women's Suffrage: The Reform Against Nature*, James, then twenty-seven, took the issue of women's equality seriously.[39] Although he dismissed Bushnell's volume as foolish, he recommended that Mill's book be read by "every one who cares in the least degree for social questions,—and who does not?—in its original form."

James refuted Bushnell's argument that women must stay out of politics if they are to retain their femininity. If femininity is as deeply ingrained as the sexists contend it is, James stated, women will not easily lose it; if they lack it, there is no excuse to prevent them from entering public life. Although generally an advocate of asceticism, he repudiated the view that women are somehow ennobled by suffering the pain of discrimination and exclusion from public life. He rejected Bushnell's examples of women's disastrous meddling with politics; the examples truly serve as arguments in favor of educating women politically and giving them the feeling of responsibility. "The strongest of all 'women's-rights' arguments is, that women are frivolous because they are irresponsible."

James's criticisms of Mill in the review reveal that James's impulses to gender-bending either emerged in his mature thinking or were uncon-scious. Since this section of the review is James's fullest explicit statement on gender roles, and anticipates contemporary debates about "essential-ism," i.e., the attribution of fixed traits either to all human beings or to particular races, genders, or ethnicities, I will quote it at length. James ac-cused Mill of becoming so passionate that "in one or two places" he pressed

> his arguments beyond the point at which, in a subject that he looked at more coolly, he would probably have stopped: as when, for example, he maintains that we are at present all but absolutely ignorant of the true mental characteristics of woman. It even makes him guilty of something like special pleading, as where he attempts to show that we have no good ground for thinking women to be naturally less fitted for original production in music than men. In fact there runs through the whole book a sort of quibble on the expression "*nature* of women." The main-stay of his thesis is, that there is nothing fixed in character, but that it may, through the education of a sufficient number of genera-tions, be produced of any quality to meet the demand; yet nevertheless he keeps speaking of woman's present condition as a distorted and "un-natural" one. "Undesirable" is the only word he can consistently use. [Mill should be able to concede, without threatening his larger point, that men and women have significantly different capacities today, even if these result from custom rather than nature.] As it is, his somewhat nervous anxiety to efface even the present distinction leads him into extremes where numbers—even of those who fully sympathize with his practical aims—will not care to follow.

> The "woman question" has hitherto been in the main a practical one. The etiolated and stunted condition of single women on the one hand, and the interests of order in the family on the other, have been the chief points of attack by the reformers, and retort by the conservatives. [The most "noteworthy feature" of Mill's book] is its thorough hostility to the accepted sentimental ideal of the personal intercourse of man and wife. [The conditions of women are not as bad in the United States as they are in England.] Much of what he attacks exists here but in feeble form. The legal abuses are in large measure obsolete; the ele-

ment of brutality which he makes so prominent in the masculine feeling of superiority is foreign; American husbands are as a rule less sensitive about their wives occupying a position of independent publicity than those of whom Mr. Mill writes. . . . [Mill's lack of support for the sentimental ideal] furnishes that intense contempt for our actual arrangements which gives such a headlong character to his work.

At the heart of those arrangements is the nuclear family with a male breadwinner. A man's illusions of security, repose, respect, and authority require a family that needs him, James postulated, especially a dependent wife. In other words, the independence and public activity that he recognized as good for women conflicts with men's emotional needs.

However he might shrink from expressing it in naked words, the wife his heart more or less subtly craves is at bottom a dependent being. In the outer world he can only hold good his position by dint of reconquering it afresh every day: life is a struggle where success is only relative, and all sanctity is torn off of him; where failure and humiliation, the exposure of weaknesses, and the unmasking of pretence, are assured incidents; and he accordingly longs for one tranquil spot where he shall be valid absolutely and once for all; where, having been accepted, he is secure from further criticism, and where his good aspirations may be respected no less than if they were accomplished realities. In a word, the elements of security and repose are essential to his ideal; and the question is, Are they easily attainable without some feeling of dependence on the woman's side,—without her relying on him to be her mediator with the external world,—without his activity overlapping hers and surrounding it on almost every side, so that he makes as it were the atmosphere in which she lives?

Many men will answer No, peremptorily; for instance, Dr. Bushnell.[40]

James did not endorse the cultural demand that he described, for women to sacrifice their autonomy and critical capacity in order for men to feel strong, accomplished, and protective, although he neglected to assess the price women pay in loss of self-confidence and strength because of dependence on their husbands.[41] He depicted alienation from the workplace, a world of "failure and humiliation," of powerlessness and failed aspirations, in which the family is supposed to compensate for a man's impotence in the world by being dependent upon him in the home. On the other hand, James implicitly criticized the value of autonomy that is at the heart of the traditional male ideal by revealing the sacrifice necessary to preserve male independence, which he acknowledged was a crafted illusion.

James's views on women might be clarified further by contrasting him briefly with two of his contemporaries: Theodore Roosevelt and Henry Adams. Roosevelt perfectly fits the model of macho politics targeted by feminist theorists. He tied together "the strenuous life" advocated by James, with war, imperialism, and traditional gender stereotypes. While calling for U.S. control of Hawaii, Cuba, Puerto Rico, and the Philippines, he wrote that "the man must be glad to do a man's work. . . . The woman must be the housewife, the helpmeet of the homemaker, the wide and fearless mother of many healthy children."[42] James insisted that both men and women could live the strenuous life, and he tried to break the link between it and imperialism.

Henry Adams may be seen either as a radical feminist with an essentialist view of women or as merely a different variety of sexist than the bellicose Roosevelt. Unlike Roosevelt and James, Adams believed that the United States needed, not more manliness, but more femininity. He characterized the politicians, industrialists, and adventurers who dominated the country as hyper-masculine. Indicting the United States for its suppression of feminine power, which he associated with love, beauty, family, and sex, Adams identified with women and hoped that the country would eventually become a place "that sensitive and timid natures could regard without a shudder."[43] Whereas Adams conceived of America as being insufficiently feminine, James believed it to be insufficiently masculine. Adams admired traditional femininity more than James did and asserted that America should change, not women. Adams feared that women would become masculine, but James welcomed that prospect. They both agreed that the United States had weakened women and gave them too small a role in post–Civil War political culture.

What has been revealed so far about James's attitudes toward women? Although retaining the idea that there might be differences between men and women, even if those differences are not permanent and implanted by nature, James criticized the constrictions of gender roles and endorsed women's public action, work, and physical activity. Although he linked his ideal of heroism with the word "manliness" and rejected passivity as "feminine," he encouraged women to be "manly." With regard to the sociological function of the family, it fulfilled the need to have others depend on men and served as a refuge from a world of work in which most people are disposable. Having outlined James's explicit attitudes about gender, the question remains, How did his attitudes affect his theory of action?

# III

James's model of heroic action could be labeled "ascetic," a term used disparagingly by some feminist theorists. In order to feel a sense of accomplishment, James believed that people must encounter danger and resistance, but he also asserted that those situations need to be balanced by repose, relaxation, and security.[44] Opposing the post–Industrial Revolution cultural norm of the driven capitalist, James's ideal encompasses a combination of hard work and vacations. The appalling aspect of poverty, according to James, is not its difficulty but the fact that no opportunity exists for relief; this aspect is galling because at the same time many people enjoy soft, easy lives and never experience the challenges faced by the poor.[45]

The ascetic character of James's model of action is found in his description of human instincts, and the main source for determining James's view of instinct is *The Principles of Psychology*. He described so many contradictory human proclivities that it is difficult to label him as an essentialist.[46] He identified as instincts hunting, fighting, envy, ambition, acquisitiveness, privacy, shyness or reserve, and modesty. He posited that human beings innately desire certainty, creativity, excitement, risk, power, development of talents, leadership, mastery, personal isolation, and sociability.[47] People have a sexual instinct, but they also have an antisex instinct, which is revealed when they recoil from being touched or by their reaction when they sit on a chair that is still warm after being occupied by someone else.[48] James's account of human instincts is ambiguous, i.e., it does not conform to traditional stereotypes of male and female.

To the extent that people are by nature aggressive, James implied, our instincts must be suppressed and channeled by institutions and reason; otherwise, society will be destroyed through war.[49] Such instincts can only be regulated, never completely repressed, which is not all bad because some elements of aggression should be preserved for the good of society.[50] Although sharing many of the same ideals, James repudiated those socialists, pacifists, and feminists who strove to eliminate manly or warlike instincts; not only was that task impossible, but accomplishing it would deprive the community of the energy necessary for public action.[51] "Martial virtues," James insisted, "are absolute and permanent human goods."[52] Although himself a pacifist, James believed that war's expression of the aggressive instinct had a healthy psychological effect that nonviolence could imitate and use for constructive purposes.[53] War brings out heroism, endurance, self-discipline, and energy; James asked how these characteristics could be developed without war.[54]

Asceticism in James's theory takes the form of self-discipline, control over emotions, resistance to pain, the acceptance without bitterness of failure and material simplicity, and a willingness to sacrifice one's interests and even one's life for the public good. Cowardice, laziness, withdrawal, and aggression have to be overcome. "Be systematically ascetic or heroic in little unnecessary points, do every day or two something for no other reason than that you would rather not do it."[55] For James, emotions must be controlled by reason, because feelings, emotions, and instincts have no inherently moral content and cannot be trusted to guide action reliably.[56]

James would be wrong, and emotions would not require policing, if there were some "natural" morality in our emotional makeup. Perhaps people instinctively hate to see their fellow creatures suffer pain, as most people are moved by stories of murder, torture, starvation, rape, and even mistreatment of animals. But if sympathy is "natural," people who hurt others would have to repress something in themselves through ideology or psychological disorder. And what can explain the widespread popularity of boxing, football, and hockey; graphically violent films; and cock fights, bull fights, and pit bull fights? Does their popularity manifest a "natural" sadistic pleasure in witnessing pain—showing that many people are deaf to the cries of others and even take pleasure in hearing those cries—or does their popularity represent cultural conditioning?[57] Are controlled sports in any sense related to larger instances of sadistic evil such as death camps, the slaughter and rape of Muslims in Bosnia, the hacking of opponents by the Tonton Macoutes in Haiti? I am not suggesting that the people who enjoy violent sports and movies are responsible for or connected with social violence, but I am endeavoring to make sense of James's assertion that the "free play" of human instincts would not create a generous, loving society. Cruelty and pleasure in the pain of others seems so prevalent that James appears to be correct in viewing instincts as being multiple and thus in need of shaping and control by society.[58]

Impulses toward violence, cruelty, and revenge have profound political implications. In a cycle of revenge, one person stabs another to compensate for past wrongs of the enemy group. The friends of the new victim react with rage. That rage should be suppressed by the individual's reason and conscience if possible but by external force if necessary. Once the violent acts are halted, the emotions may eventually be calmed so that a peace process can begin. James hoped that reason—thinking things out, cooling down, considering the consequences of one's action—would produce moral action. In short, his ideal of action rejects aggressive action while demanding control over emotions. Wolin comments on this point: "What is James presupposing in the way of conditions so that weighing things out would produce moral action? It seems to me that fresh from nearly a half century of debate over slavery there is a limit to what one can expect from this kind of counsel. And one would also want to ask if there are no circumstances under which rage is not only natural but even commendable." I would reply that democratic debate becomes difficult when one or both parties are enraged.

James's asceticism includes the belief that people need to accept failure and modest levels of material comfort. "The more one thinks about the demands of participatory life," muses Wolin, "the more one sees that they are at odds with the things that James is pointing to: the success ethic, materialism, and the comfort ethic." Unlike Machiavelli, James does not insist that fate must always be dominated, and this willingness to relinquish control over fate could be seen as an implicit critique of mastery as a male ideal.[59] James counseled that while the American worship of "the bitch-goddess SUCCESS . . . is our national disease," failure in most human enterprises is inevitable, and we need to learn to fail gracefully.[60] "It seems almost as if it were necessary to become worthless as a practical being . . . [like] your mystic, your dreamer, or your insolvent tramp or loafer" in order to gain perspective on a nation's values. People who win at the game rarely question its validity.[61] Poverty is taken to be a dishonorable badge of failure, but James proposed that if it comes, poverty should be accepted without a feeling of humiliation. In fact, living modestly offers political actors freedom because they need not dread loss of possessions.

> Think of the strength which personal indifference to poverty would give us if we were devoted to unpopular causes. We need no longer hold our tongues or fear to vote the revolutionary or reformatory ticket. Our stocks might fall, our hopes of promotion vanish, our salaries stop, our club doors close in our faces; yet, while we lived, we would imperturbably bear witness to the spirit, and our example would help to set free our generation.[62]

Simple living makes freely chosen action more likely.[63] At the other end of the financial spectrum, some people with great wealth seek legislation that benefits the poor without facing the danger of joining their ranks. Such noblesse oblige is, of course, exceptional.

James's ascetic ideal was not only offered for a few heroes. Indeed, he advised that no one should seek only material luxury; all should pursue deeds that demand risk.[64] But to do so does not always mean extraordinary accomplishments. In a world frequently subjected to war, genocide, violent crime, and famine, achieving a modest level of security is often a heroic act. James would go further and insist that considerable courage and strength are required to remain sane, moral, and engaged with the world while enduring the typical boredom and indignities of the workplace, frustrations of traffic jams and bureaucratic foul-ups, the distress and pain of illness, the sickness and death of a loved one, and witnessing, even via the media, the suffering of others.[65] James made this point most clearly in a response to a speech by his friend Oliver Wendell Holmes, in which Holmes had suggested that everyone should strive to be heroic.[66] In a private letter, James bemoaned the fact that Holmes

> celebrate(s) mere vital excitement, *la joie de vivre*, as a protest against humdrum solemnity. But to make it systematic, and oppose it, as an ideal and a duty, to the ordinarily recognized duties, is to pervert it altogether. . . . It is curiously childish to me, and Wendell always forgets

that on his own terms the dutiful people also fulfil his law. Even they live hard, and enjoy the struggle with their opposing devils! So let them alone! . . . Mere excitement is an immature ideal.[67]

James might appear to be contradictory here: if heroism is pervasive, why did he elsewhere condemn American softness and appeal for a moral equivalent of war?[68] James found heroic strength in everyday life, which is the opposite of softness. His objection was to the rise of large government, created in response to utopian visions, that would supplant the initiatives of communities and individuals.

James invited citizens to become more energetic in the face of increasingly powerful institutions in the late nineteenth century, but he also demanded respect for the lives of ordinary citizens. That respect led James to proportional demands from the citizenry, a version of "from each according to their ability." For some people, attaining the bare necessities of life or holding onto a job requires a heroic struggle, and they are not obligated to undertake extraordinary public action beyond fulfilling the minimal civic duties. But the elite, who possess economic or emotional security, including the Victorian single woman of the middle class, should push themselves to accomplish more and give more to the community. Not everyone has the same task; the economic and intellectual elites are held to a higher standard. James believed that "there must be *novelty* in an ideal— novelty at least for him whom the ideal grasps. Sodden routine is incompatible with ideality, although what is sodden routine for one person may be ideal novelty for another."[69]

James condemned Teddy Roosevelt for being too abstract, saying of his imperialist rhetoric:

Although in middle life, as the years age, and in a situation of responsibility concrete enough, he is still mentally in the Sturm and Drang period of early adolescence, treats human affairs . . . from the sole point of view of the organic excitement and difficulty they may bring, gushes over war as the ideal condition of human society, for the manly strenuousness which it involves, and treats peace as a condition of blubberlike and swollen ignobility, fit only for huckstering weaklings, dwelling in gray twilight and heedless of the higher life. Not a word of the cause—one foe is as good as another.[70]

James censured Roosevelt for his abstract call to action, blaming him for blindness to the fact that action takes its moral content from its cause. Similarly, he reproached Roosevelt with the same criticism he leveled at Holmes: the constant call for struggle and risk as the essence of courage. "In both cases," Wolin comments, "he is trying to deal with a certain kind of immaturity on their part, a juvenile quality, in which excitement appears to be a substitute for thought." James may have at certain points appeared guilty of the very things for which he chided Roosevelt and Holmes, but those criticisms reveal that he recognized the problem of endorsing action as a universal good.

Wendy Brown attempts, unsuccessfully I think, to clarify the difference between masculine and "postmasculinist" courage when she states that courage has been narrowly defined by men as establishing one's humanness by overcoming the instinctual fear of death. She wishes to keep courage but remove its macho elements. "A post-masculinist politics must [not] refuse a place to bold, impetuous, forceful or daring actions."[71] Feminist courage, according to Brown, would sustain life, risk one's identity, and engage with others in relationships of trust.[72] Although James might not have understood the concept of risking one's identity, he probably would not otherwise have objected to Brown's formulation, other than to ask if feminist theorists need to recognize, and do something other than repress, the widespread impulses of aggression and competition ("universal and competitive passion") that James hoped to transmute into "civic passion."[73]

Courage is a central element in political action. Radical action usually demands the strength to think independently of prevailing ideas and then the fortitude to accept suffering and even death in resisting power.[74] Whatever the joys and material benefits of political action, if people act on their ideals, they might be disappointed, condemned by family and friends, fired from their jobs, physically attacked, incarcerated, and even killed. Bravery is required to resist the prevailing views and customs of one's family, community, or country, and until one finds friends and comrades it can be a lonely effort.[75]

The vocabulary of gender in relationship to courage now seems outmoded. Feminist theorists correctly teach that one should not enter politics to test one's power and endurance; such testing seems more appropriate to physical training, solo sports, and wilderness adventure. Even though some feminist theorists have argued that masculine courage overvalues autonomy, the actual concept and experience of courage have been more complex. Politics has never overvalued autonomy because action has always required trust; although unions have frequently been dominated by men, union leaders preach solidarity. And trust, particularly in war, is a traditional component of courage: "Be there for your buddy." Feminists have rightly indicted those people who say that only men can be brave. Some men may have mistakenly postulated that only they have the capacity for true courage, and James did associate courage with "manliness," but he never claimed that only men could possess it. He quite appropriately muddied the waters.

Thinking about gender, courage, and muddied water reminds me of a rafting trip I took in Utah in the summer of 1995 through the perilous Cataract Canyon of the Colorado River. The woman who guided our eighteen-foot oar boat, which carried three passengers and lots of gear, had long thick brown hair and powerful legs and arms. There was nothing masculine about her. As we went through the rapids at Big Drop Two, she missed an intended cut, and the raft flipped. All four of us were dumped into the freezing water. The guide got caught by the ropes under the boat and wounded her hand, finally cutting herself loose just in time to breathe again. Coming up, she told me to push her onto the overturned raft and then helped me climb onto it before handing me over to a rescue boat, telling them to make sure I got warm. She stayed on top of the raft through the rest of the rapids. When we talked later, she was careful to admit that something frightening and dangerous had happened. Although she had flipped before, she had never done so while carrying passengers and had never been in such personal difficulty. She quietly vowed that if she could not get people safely through the rapids—all of us made it—she would quit. (She wrote me later that she went back through Cataract Canyon several more times that summer, flipping again but "more cleanly.") I was impressed with her bravery, skill, and strength (no match for the river that day), as well as her honesty and concern for others. This is a long way of saying that I admired her courage, and James would have admired her, and that admiration has little to do with gender. It was neither masculine nor feminine, just courage itself.[76]

# IV

James's model of action should not be dismissed because there is much good in it. Politics still requires bravery. In an age when many people believe that capitalism has triumphed over all possible alternatives, there remains a need for voices that esteem the common good over the pursuit of private interest. Following James would not lead to a greater war against nature even if his misleading words called for that. He desired neither deforestation with electric chain saws nor chemical pollution of the water and air; his examples of the war against nature include the building of homes, the repairing of roads, feeding the hungry, and developing a robust character by challenging ourselves in nature. Both men and women can do all of those things.[77] Despite his vocabulary, James did not have a gender-specific definition of action, and he indicated that women are as capable of political virtue as men.

The question then becomes, Does James's model of action foster in men and women an aggressive, hyper-masculine character? I sympathize with Henry Adams's desire to protect "timid natures." Is there sufficient room in James's ideal for people who are gentle, soft, and shy, qualities once associated with women? We might be inclined to agree with James when he demanded of Holmes, Leave the shy people alone! There is a political problem with such a stance. Can gentleness be accepted in a radical democracy if each citizen is expected to take part in political action and politics requires a thick skin? If democracy does demand a certain type of temperament, one worries about the coercion necessary to create that temperament and the type of character that might be lost. This worry may be quite fantastic since most personalities are rendered passive and silent by bureaucracies and undemocratic forms of power in schools, the workplace, and government; participatory democracy promises to fulfill far more human potentialities than it would frustrate.[78]

A second political issue raised by the ideal of robustness is that, as Hartsock suggested, such an ideal might easily become aggressive and burst the boundaries of law and civility. James did not create aggression, but he acknowledged it and called for channeling it away from violence, imperialism, and war into sports, wilderness adventure, and contributions to the public good such as teaching in inner-city schools, joining a union, or risking one's life by working with gangs or escorting women and doctors into abortion clinics. Although the manly ideal might degenerate into violence, violence is not the usual result of political actors behaving in the vigorous manner prescribed by James. The real problem with James's military metaphors for citizenship is their conception of authority as command and obedience. "Martial virtues must be the enduring cement," James avowed in a passage quoted earlier in Chapter 2, "intrepidity, contempt of softness, surrender of private interest, *obedience to command*, must still remain the rock on which states are built."[79] The relationship of citizens to rulers is not that of soldiers to their commanders, a relationship that may be justified under conditions of war but offers no standard for democracies in which leaders should be questioned as well as followed. There are models of authority appropriate to a democratic community, the chief criterion of which is that authority encourage independent thinking and action on the part of the citizens, but the regular, rarely questioned obedience of military life is not one of those models.

Finally, the question must be raised whether gender categories any longer make sense in discussing political action. Borrowing a theoretical device employed by political theorist Hanna Pitkin, one might ask what the difference is between manly action "at its best," as described by someone like James or Arendt, and feminist action at its best, as described by someone like Pitkin or Brown? Both sides appeal for risk, vigor, courage, and contribution to the community. Feminist theory and the action of thousands of courageous women have resulted in genuine progress so that women and men need no longer meet arbitrary standards of masculinity and femininity. James's ambiguity and encouragement of women may have added a bit to this progress. Freed from gender specificity, a term that does not quite fit James, his advocacy of action constitutes an addition to democratic theory despite the dated and unnecessarily gender-laden vocabulary he employed. Democratic citizenship requires of all citizens the vigor, courage, and self-discipline advocated by James.

*Chapter 3*

# Sources of Respect

I

Sustaining friendly relationships among citizens as they resolve their disputes democratically requires mutual respect. Justice Learned Hand interpreted "the spirit of liberty" as "the spirit which seeks to understand the minds of other men and women."[1] Without some degree of unity among individuals and groups, politics—the peaceful resolution of conflict—breaks down and differences are resolved, if at all, by the weaker yielding to the superior power. Unity's effects might be attained by suppressing disagreements or invoking a hegemonic identity ("to be a good citizen you must believe this and practice that"), or, and this ideal is far more difficult to achieve, genuine unity could be created by encouraging citizens to cherish their commonalities and to esteem people of different colors, religions, classes, income levels, degrees of power, genders, ideologies, and sexual preferences. One could imagine the following exhortation, "By virtue of our citizenship in this country, we share a common past, laws, language, and institutions, although we also belong to particular groups with unique histories, customs, and languages, that make distinctive contributions to the collectivity."[2]

The historical context in which William James thought about these matters is significantly similar to the present. U.S. foreign policy frequently manifests the racism and xenophobia that James saw in U.S. interventions in Cuba, the Philippines, Venezuela, and Haiti,[3] and at home, there are echoes of the intense class warfare of the late nineteenth century; flashpoints for hostility then and now include race, religion, region, gender, sexuality, and ideology. Just as immigrants from Germany, Eastern Europe, and Ireland once altered the ethnic composition of the United States, a corresponding transformation is now occurring as a result of immigration from Mexico, Central America, Cuba, Africa, and Asia. Cuban immi-

54

grants clash with African Americans in Miami for political power, and the tension between blacks and Jews has been intense since the demise of the civil rights movement. In Crown Heights, Brooklyn, blacks and Orthodox Jews battle for scarce city resources that neither control, and in 1994 a prominent Yale historian of slavery chose not to speak at Howard University because he feared anti-Semitic heckling.[4]

Racial, religious, and ethnic tensions are expressed in ideological debates over affirmative action, the means of fairly representing minorities in Congress, the content of school curricula, and the use of languages other than English in education and public affairs. Clashes over homosexuality have been waged more openly than ever before in schools, the military, and street assaults on gays and lesbians, and a women's educational and cultural retreat started by two lesbians in Mississippi became an armed camp in response to threats from hostile neighbors.[5] In reaction to the decline of culturally sanctioned truths and a multiplicity of perspectives, some political and religious movements express their positions as indisputable and nonnegotiable. The militia movement, neo-Nazis, Black Muslims, and certain fundamentalist Jewish and Islamic sects combine absolutism, hatred, and violence. Women have been murdered in Algeria for not wearing the veil.[6] Even "moderates" divide the world into the righteous and the damned: some of the groups just listed have become pariahs for the rest of us.[7]

Given the fact that previous grounds of unity—such as respect for law or acquiescence to hierarchies dominated by whites, males, and Protestants—are eroding, will domestic conflicts become increasingly violent? Will the United States go the way of Algeria, Egypt, and the former Yugoslavia? The Los Angeles riots, terrorist bombings, and attacks on abortion clinics are worrisome signs.

What institutions, customs, ideology, or temperament could unify or at least dampen the hostility in our diverse society? All answers to that question will meet with skepticism. One consequence of the philosophic dispute over relativism and subjectivism (does truth exist outside of individual or cultural preference and self-interest?) has been the abandonment of the old ideal of neutrality, i.e., one should and can find a position untainted by interest that represents the common good. Today, every claim made in the name of the common good is exposed for its selfish interests or will to power.[8]

The Federalist founders claimed to have discovered a substitute for unity: divide the people so that no one faction can predominate while increasing the scale of government and using checks and balances to distance political institutions from popular will.[9] The powerful, centralized state fills one function of unity when it suppresses conflict through the army, police, courts, and incarceration system. Madisonian means of resolving discord are less available to direct democracies; refusing to transfer power to the state gives citizens more personal responsibility and requires them to enter into political relationships with fellow citizens.[10] A democracy cannot abolish disagreements or strong feelings among citizens, but both must be tempered if they are not to erupt into violence.

The United States has resources in its theoretical and political traditions to help in the creation of a multicultural society in which groups negotiate their differences without demonizing each other. According to literary critic Giles Gunn:

> While pragmatic criticism advocates no particular policies, it does possess a specifiable politics. It is a politics distinguished by the democratic preference for rendering differences conversable so that the conflicts they produce, instead of being destructive of human community, can be potentially creative of it; can broaden and thicken public culture rather than depleting it.[11]

It may not be much of an exaggeration to say that the pragmatic criticism described by Gunn was largely invented by William James, although he went beyond Gunn's ideals to delineate the kinds of conditions, prerequisites, and behaviors that are needed in order to render differences conversable.

James exemplified mutual respect, sometimes even embarrassing his friends with his openness to advocates of eccentric causes such as parapsychology. In an obituary that identified democracy with egalitarian tolerance, Walter Lippmann declared that James

> was simply keeping America's promise: he was actually doing what we, as a nation, proclaimed that we would do. He was tolerant; he was willing to listen to what seems preposterous, and to consider what might, though queer, be true. And he showed that this democratic

attitude of mind is every bit as fruitful as the aristocratic determination to ignore new and strange-looking ideas. James was a democrat. He gave all men and all creeds, any idea, any theory, any superstition, a respectful hearing. . . . It is an encouraging thought that America should have produced perhaps the most tolerant man of our generation.[12]

W. E. B. Du Bois revered James for being first among Harvard's transformative national intellectual leaders, "unshackled in thought and custom who were beating back bars of ignorance and particularism and prejudice."[13]

Perfect harmony was not James's ideal; he believed that conflict was healthy. So he did not endeavor, even at the level of theory, to discourage the social struggles of late-nineteenth-century American society, but in order to preserve democratic institutions, he sought to reduce hatred and misconceptions in confrontations between capital and labor, natives and immigrants, blacks and whites, men and women.[14] In protesting U.S. intervention in the Philippines and Cuba and condemning the Spanish-American War, James wanted to curb the feelings of superiority toward other countries that fueled American imperialism.[15] Not only does imperialism violate abstract principles of right, but James believed that tolerance and self-determination are embodied in the Declaration of Independence, and thus constitutive of the American political spirit, and imperialism corrupts that spirit.

In analyzing the causes of corruption, James did not find fault with either liberalism or American political institutions, which at their best preserve liberty. Grasping social psychology shaped by ideologies and values, leadership and social structures, was for James crucial to exposing the root of the problem. In despair over the Spanish-American War, James said:

Seriously speaking, this whole business has thrown a most instructive light on the way in which history is made, and has illustrated to perfection the *psychologie des foules* [crowd psychology]! The basis of it all is, or rather was, perfectly honest humanitarianism, and an absolutely disinterested desire on the part of our people to set the Cubans free. . . . On this, various interests worked for their purposes in favor of war.[16]

He identified a common source of domestic political violence and imperialism: both result, at least in part, from a "blindness" that creates contempt for cultures and outlooks other than one's own. He analyzed the causes of this blindness and indicated an approach to overcoming it.

II

James's conception of mutual respect combined tolerance, based on the faith that others are equal in value and possess a share of truth, with the conviction that failure to perceive this equality results from an inevitable cultural process. If incognizance is impossible to dispel, every effort should be made to withhold judgment. "International comparisons are a great waste of time—at any rate, international judgments and the passing of sentences are. Every nation has ideals and difficulties and sentiments which are an impenetrable secret to one not of the blood. Let them alone, let each one work out its salvation on its own lines."[17] James specified the greatest danger to other cultures as being imperiousness, arguing that we must not

> be forward in pronouncing on the meaninglessness of forms of existence other than our own; and [the result of the inquiry into the causes of blindness] commands us to tolerate, respect, and indulge those whom we see harmlessly interested and happy in their own ways, however unintelligible these may be to us. Hands off: neither the whole of truth, nor the whole of good, is revealed to any single observer, although each observer gains a partial superiority of insight from the peculiar position in which he stands.[18]

James's tolerance was not anarchic; he insisted that antagonists should remain within the boundaries of the law. American democracy is based on

> two inveterate habits carried into public life. . . . They can never be too often pointed out or praised. One of them is the habit of trained and disciplined good temper towards the opposite party when it fairly wins its innings—it was by breaking from this habit the slave States nearly wrecked our Nation. The other is that of fierce and merciless

resentment towards every man or set of men who break the public peace—it was by holding to this habit the free States saved her life.[19]

One might wonder if James here reveals that his concept of democracy is founded on the coercion feared by a postmodernist such as Connolly, but it should be remembered that James's rhetoric is colored heavily by the Civil War experience so that he was thinking not only of people who break the peace but of those who would destroy the union.[20] Commitment to democratic rules of settling disputes was, for James, one element of mutual respect along with appreciation of others, self-criticism, and an acknowledgment of an innate inability to fathom others fully.

Mutual respect is the ideal relationship among citizens in a democracy, but we need not go to democratic dreamland: to respect every position— for example, to deny that the Holocaust occurred or to posit the genetic inferiority of African Americans—is to sanction evil. *New Yorker* critic Adam Gopnick parodied a mad objectivity that could be confused with mutual respect:

> You sometimes have the depressing feeling that if the Beer Hall Putsch took place in America today there would be an investigation in the news magazines of Hitler's claim ("Though Hitler's charge that Jews control the media remains unproved, it has sparked a welcome debate on the relationships between Jews and other Germans. In the long run, this may be the best thing to come from this miserable incident").[21]

James placed limits on tolerance:

> The first thing to learn in intercourse with others is non-interference with their own peculiar ways of being happy, *provided those ways do not assume to interfere by violence with ours.* No one has insight into all the ideals. No one should presume to judge them off-hand. The pretension to dogmatize about them in each other is the root of most human injustices and cruelties, and the trait in human character most likely to make the angels weep.[22]

Democratic action requires mutual respect because it makes peaceful disagreement viable. Mutual respect implies a friendly attitude toward one's fellow citizens, including political opponents. That friendly attitude includes a theory of truth, a tendency to dismiss hierarchies as indicators of who merits respect, and an appreciation for the variety of contributions made by various people in a society.

In certain moods, James professed that virtually everyone detects part of the truth and no one apprehends the whole.[23] A stranger's ideas, way of life, character, or culture probably have something worthy in them that we often cannot recognize since they differ from our own portion of the truth. One therefore should strive to observe the world, especially in a confrontation, from the other's point of view, even learning from them if possible. "Respect has to be treated as a very difficult demand because in a society where you emphasize toleration of diversity you are going to have to do a lot of respecting," remarks Wolin. "That is more than simply the type of respect one must show in personal relationships. Respect is strained when one has all kinds of groups, ideologies, and interests to think about, with all their various spokespersons. And that also makes it difficult to see the world from their point of view because in the context of differences you've often got a bewildering variety of points of view."[24]

James opposed our common tendency to designate the voices of some groups as worth hearing while ignoring others altogether. Some people turn deaf ears to women, blacks, the working class, New Age devotees, evangelists, politicians, professors, and journalists. Some accept nothing as true if it cannot be validated by mainstream science. For example, in a reversal of common sentiments, the father of a friend of mine was so convinced by a study he had read of marijuana's benefits that he refused to acknowledge, even when it was described to him from experience, the damaging effects of his own son's addiction to the drug. In contrast, James tried to listen to everyone, including advocates of weird theories and partisans of lost causes, with an open mind.

To engage James on this issue requires confronting an ancient problem in political theory: What is the value of a citizen? From the standpoint of the community, are all citizens of the same worth? Do they deserve the same rewards? In *The Politics*, Aristotle contended that "the good in the sphere of politics is justice; and justice consists in what tends to promote the common interest. General opinion makes it consist in some sort of equality. . . . [I]t considers that persons who are equal should have assigned to them equal things. . . . [Y]es; but equals and unequals *in what?*"

(bk. 3, chap. 12, 1–2). Superior people should receive superior rewards, but Aristotle asks what makes a superior person. Surely not complexion or height. He concludes that "claims to political rights must be based on the ground of contribution to the elements which constitute the being of the state. There is thus good ground for the claims to honour and office which are made by persons of good descent, free birth, or wealth" (bk. 3, chap. 12, 8). He rejects the assertion, which he labels "democratic," that the people who are equal in one thing should have an equal share of all things (bk. 3, chap. 13, 1).[25]

James may have come close to Aristotle's formulation in holding that while everyone can and should make a contribution to the country, those contributions are of different worth. He tried to avoid esteeming exclusively the working class or the elite. He favorably quoted Tolstoy's praise for those at the bottom of society—"If I could show you these men and women, all the world over, in every stage of history, under every abuse of error, under every circumstance of failure, without hope, without help, without thanks, still obscurely fighting the lost fight of virtue, still clinging to some rag of honour, the poor jewel of their souls!"—and responded:

All this is as true as it is splendid and terribly do we need our Tolstois and Stevensons to keep our sense for it alive. . . . [Yet] Tolstoi overcorrect[s] our social prejudices, when he makes his love of the peasant so exclusive, and hardens his heart towards the educated man as absolutely as he does. . . . Is it so certain that the surroundings and circumstances of the virtue do make so little difference in the importance of the result? Is the functional utility, the worth to the universe of a certain definite amount of courage, kindliness, and patience, no greater if the possessor of these virtues is in an educated situation, working out far-reaching tasks, than if he be an illiterate nobody, hewing wood and drawing water, just to keep himself alive? Tolstoi's philosophy, deeply enlightening though it certainly is, remains a false abstraction. It savors too much of that oriental pessimism and nihilism of his, which declares the whole phenomenal world and its facts and their distinctions to be a cunning fraud.[26]

One discerns in this approach to equality James's odd mixture of egalitarianism and patrician arrogance, radical critique of and respect for the status quo. James called for an appreciation of both the workers' and the non-workers' contributions. Intelligence, intellectual innovation, vigor, character, and occupation all are significant, James insisted. Yet great skill and courage in brain surgery or diplomacy are more praiseworthy than the same attributes in plumbing, essential as the latter might be. This is the point at which James broke with Tolstoy, who came to value the life and work of peasants while condemning every other type of life, including the novelist's. James's individualism led him to add that one's place, occupation, membership, dress, and wealth are not certain indicators of merit, which should be judged not solely on the type of contribution one makes but on the effort one expends to make it as well.[27]

The acceptance of inequality erodes the democratic temperament and replaces it with passivity. We have grown accustomed to hierarchies in everyday life: bosses, owners, boards of directors, and the wealthy give orders to the managers, workers, and secretaries who carry them out. All people are allowed to vote and receive a fair trial, which perpetuates the legitimating illusion of equal power despite the grinding reality of inequality. Marx articulated the essence of the situation: "The state abolishes, after its fashion, the distinctions established by *birth, social rank, education, occupation,* when it decrees that birth, social rank, education, occupation are *non-political* distinctions; when it proclaims, without regard to these distinctions, that every member of society is an *equal* partner in popular sovereignty."[28] Despite freedom to criticize the state, you disagree with the boss at your peril, particularly if you lack tenure or a union contract. In a participatory democracy, legal equality, even as an ideal, is insufficient: the goal should be to equalize power both in politics and in everyday life.

Such equalization is both a condition and a result of mutual respect. You would not attempt to give your fellow citizens power unless you had a generous attitude toward them. James did not appeal for the transformation of the United States into a radical democracy, but his commitment to mutual respect and participation is in the spirit of radical democracy. A political meaning of "respect" might be as follows: Even if I disagree with your views and work against their realization, I will try not to hate you. I will try to fathom your way of viewing the world and will think about what you say rather than punish you for speaking your ideas or ignore the fact that you have spoken.[29]

A disrespectful teacher ignores or openly disdains the comments of students. The recommendation that every person should be heard runs counter to the idea that only a few people matter because of their education, wealth, color, or status. Philosopher Maurice Natanson expressed something like this, during an interview, in discussing his teacher Alfred Schutz:

> I learned a lot about human existence from Schutz precisely in terms of what's at issue when you're dealing with another person. And at one point he told me, "Natanson, these are *human beings*." You say, "Well, Professor So-and-So's done this, and this person's done that; there's this quarrel and that difficulty." But basically it isn't whether the paper was given the right grade, or whether you did the right thing, or the position you took was this, that or the other. It was basically that you're dealing with persons, and that's what I came to realize.[30]

Natanson's formulation implies, as does a theory of radical democracy, that people have intrinsic worth despite criticisms of them and regardless of their social roles.

In a democracy, each citizen is entrusted with some power to decide the direction of the polity, and therefore citizens are not nonentities and are more than possible converts or political targets; potentially, they are one's teachers. According to Gandhi and Martin Luther King, Jr., while working for change we should try to sympathize with and even love our opponents. King preached, "The Christian virtues of love, mercy and forgiveness should stand at the center of our lives." Love of one's enemies "might well be the salvation of our civilization."[31] Even though respecting someone does not require liking them or admiring them, creating respect is still a political goal. Christopher Lasch disagrees:

> We are determined to respect everyone, but we have forgotten that respect has to be earned. Respect is not another word for tolerance. . . . Respect is what we experience in the presence of admirable achievements, admirably formed characters, natural gifts put to good use. It entails the exercise of discriminating judgment, not indiscriminate acceptance.[32]

I appreciate Lasch's use of "respect" but cannot completely accept it because democracy is built on respect of a certain kind for everyone—even the unpleasant, the unlearned, the untalented, and the failed.[33]

It is hard to define what kind of respect. One wants to avoid deprecating all those with whom one disagrees without pretending to "respect" every person and position no matter how wicked. In commenting on the manuscript version of this book, Carey McWilliams proposed that democratic respect may lie in holding everyone accountable to the appropriate standards. This idea seems plausible until one encounters a bizarre theory of respect in an prominent American public policy text, Mickey Kaus's *The End of Equality*.[34] Kaus believes "social equality" as a goal is superior to "monetary equality" because of the impossibility and negative effects of redistributing wealth, whereas social equality would guarantee that people are respected regardless of their income. He then details as appropriate standards for respect work, politeness, and the fulfillment of obligations; in other words, people who do not work are unworthy of respect. Kaus's contempt is directed not at the idle rich or nonworking spouses in the middle and upper classes, but at the "threatening" black underclass, which he presumes would vanish in a good society. One could say that Kaus does not fairly apply his own standards or the right standards of respect, but what are the right standards for writing off people as citizens and human beings?

Christian theologians have wrestled with the same dilemma: at their worst, they have condemned to hell atheists, non-Christians, and non-church members; at their most generous, they have offered forgiveness and love to every human being no matter how low one has fallen in society or how vile one's crimes. Perhaps that latter religious goal is politically impossible because societies require common ideals, laws, and limits on membership. "If you do such and such, God may forgive you, but we cannot."

Nevertheless, countries that would be democracies must promote respect even for political opponents.[35] This attitude, in which respect permits peaceful disagreement, is illustrated by the speech of Nelson Mandela upon winning election as the first president of postapartheid South Africa.

> I would . . . like to congratulate President de Klerk for the strong showing the National Party has displayed in this election. I also want to congratulate him for the many days, weeks and months and the four

years that we have worked together, quarreled, addressed sensitive problems and at the end of our heated exchanges were able to shake hands and to drink coffee. . . . The calm and tolerant atmosphere that prevailed during the election depicts the type of South Africa we can build. . . . We might have our differences, but we are one people with a common destiny in our rich variety of culture, race and tradition.[36]

Mutual respect can be furthered by attempting to imagine the viewpoint of opposition groups and individuals. What is their history and present situation? Under what pressures do they labor? How do they interpret the controversy? Realizing that no group is monolithic, what are the lines of disagreement within that group? It may be easy in a pejorative sense to identify others' contradictions—"If they believe in peace, why do they stir up trouble?" "They oppose abortion because it destroys life but they support the National Rifle Association and the death penalty"—but it is more difficult to give a generous account of an adversary's position. What are the strongest, most appealing arguments to be made for the other side?[37]

The effort to comprehend is not identical to respect and toleration. Some people should be understood—neo-Nazis or members of the Ku Klux Klan, for example—if only for self-protection, but they should be neither respected nor, depending on their actions, tolerated. Toleration, when appropriate, is a minimal relationship toward others; respect is more substantial.[38] In traditional liberalism, toleration implies letting others alone; you need not consider the views of your opponents, just allow them to be expressed. You can tolerate others while ignoring them.[39] Tolerance is preferable to unjustified persecution, but respect goes further.

The difference between toleration and respect might be illustrated by imagining a college campus that for most of its history formally excluded women from the student body and restricted the number of blacks and Jews. The college might finally enroll those it once excluded or restricted yet never incorporate them into the dominant campus culture. On many campuses, virtually every public portrait is of white males, except for the occasional donor's wife, who is also white. Many cafeterias serve no food influenced by the cooking of Asia, Africa, or South America, although students at the schools come from those places. Colleges have clubs for African Americans; international students; friends of gays, lesbians, bisexuals;

and women's groups as well as sites for Hillel and the Newman society, but the dominant culture tends to remain straight, white, and male. There is toleration but not the mutual respect that would alter the character of the community.

Political action with toleration but not respect is old-fashioned pluralism: each group struggles for power; some participants are broadened by their participation, and some are affected by witnessing the activity; but little interpenetration or learning takes place among different groups in the society. Mutual respect does not demand admiration or affection; it begins with tolerance, proceeds to recognition, and continues to knowledge and transformation. James's contribution is not only to the expression of that ideal but to an analysis of the impediments to creating and attaining it.

# III

At the root of what today would be called prejudice, racism, sexism, and imperialism, James saw "blindness," by which he meant that the lives of people different from us are rarely understood or appreciated. James attempted to make contact with the ordinary and the commonplace without being overly sentimental and realizing their limitations. The search for what is common to common people, and making that into something common to us all, is a crucial element of James's democratic thinking.[40]

> I use the brief term labor-question to cover all sorts of anarchistic discontents and socialistic projects, and the conservative resistances which they provoke. So far as this conflict is unhealthy and regrettable—and I think it is so only to a limited extent—the unhealthiness consists solely in the fact that one-half of our fellow-countrymen remain entirely blind to the internal significance of the lives of the other half.[41]

If mutual respect is the ideal relationship for democratic citizens, "blindness" is the great psychological obstacle to achieving it. When a group or nation fails to see others' virtues or truths, it looks down on them, which opens the door to violence and domination. Even though the rich and middle classes share the same society, they understand neither the plight nor the contributions of the working class and the poor—and the working class and poor misperceive the bourgeoisie.

James detected this blindness in himself and, in attempting to overcome it, confessed an inability to recognize the strengths of workers. In a related admission of obtuseness, he dramatized his reaction to the cleared land called a "cove" in the North Carolina mountains:

> The impression [of the coves] on my mind was one of unmitigated squalor, but after a local resident informed him "we ain't happy here unless we are getting one of these coves under cultivation" . . . [I] instantly felt that I had been losing the whole inward significance of the situation. . . . In short, the clearing, which to me was a mere ugly picture on the retina, was to them a symbol redolent with moral memories and sang a very paean of duty, struggle, and success.[42]

James's effort to grasp what was meaningful to the Carolinians foreshadowed James Agee's attempt in *Let Us Now Praise Famous Men* to capture the inner experience of poor southern families during the Great Depression rather than portraying only their external squalor, as he had been sent to do.[43]

After designating incognizance as a major cause of social conflict and imperialism, James sought to pinpoint its causes, enumerating at least four: the origin of opinions in feelings; the tendency to transform differences into hierarchies; the emphasis on monetary success that obscures the worth of other goals; and the belief that our own views, ideals, and ways of life rest on an objective foundation.[44] I discuss the last, the relationship of truth and action, in Chapter 4. As to the first, our opinions do not flow from a rational examination of the alternatives. Instead, philosophical, religious, and political standpoints originate in personalities and feelings.[45] Reason therefore cannot be of paramount importance in overcoming blindness; hearing "reasonable" arguments against one's position will rarely produce a change. Then too, our feelings are restricted in their objects: we feel most intensely our own pain and pleasure and only empathize with those around us. The misery of having a broken leg is much worse than the reaction to hearing a report, even from a friend, of the agony of a broken leg. Generally, we care most about our own body, family, neighborhood, city or region, college or club, religion, country.[46] The further you get from the self, the more difficult it is to sympathize. The loyalties of others for their friends, pets, schools, fraternities or sororities, and causes are often perplexing.

"Ancestral" prejudice, which reifies differences among social groups, is a second cause of blindness. Although we may have once understood that human beings are essentially equal in their ability to contribute to the common good and in believing their lives to be significant or meaningful, we come to regard the people with money, status, family connections, style, or the "right" color of skin as being of a higher human order. James discovered prejudices in himself and admitted that they were directed particularly against workers and poor southerners.[47] He finally became aware that the heroism he feared to be passing out of American life is to be found in the lives of the working class—and that he had been unable to see that fact because "I had been steeping myself in pure ancestral blindness."[48]

Concerning the third cause, wealth, too, creates blindness. James posited the existence of psychological connections among blindness, capitalism, and imperialism.[49] The contempt for other cultures produced by capitalism sanctions interference. James did not quite condemn the pursuit of material success as immoral but in a Thoreauvian vein, maintained that it conceals the worth of other goals and experiences.[50] Powerfully focusing the energy of many Americans and organizing their activities and time, seeking wealth is seen as a form of nirvana—and replaces all other goals.

So blind and dead does the clamor of our own practical interests make us to all other things, that it seems almost as if it were necessary to become worthless as a practical being, if one is to hope to attain to any breadth of insight into the impersonal world of worths as such, to have any perception of life's meaning on a large objective scale. Only your mystic, your dreamer, or your insolvent tramp or loafer, can afford so sympathetic an occupation which will change the usual standards of human values in the twinkling of an eye, giving to foolishness a place ahead of power, and laying low in a minute the distinctions which it takes a hard-working conventional man a lifetime to build up. You may be a prophet at this rate; but you cannot be a worldly success.[51]

When almost all citizens are materialists, one must abandon society to appreciate ways of life organized around values other than money, success, and technological advancement.

We of the highly educated classes (so called) have most of us got far, far away from Nature. We are trained to seek the choice, the rare, the exquisite, exclusively, and to overlook the common. . . . The remedy under such conditions is to descend to a more profound and primitive level. . . . The savages and children of nature to whom we deem ourselves so much superior, certainly are alive where we are often dead . . . and could they write as glibly as we do, they would read us impressive lectures on our impatience for improvement and on our blindness to the fundamental static goods of life.[52]

James may have been substituting positive stereotypes of the "primitive" for negative ones; nevertheless, the purpose of promoting empathy with "primitives," and insinuating that "savages" have an access to truth denied to the elite of Western civilization, is to undermine the proposition used to justify American imperialism that "advanced" societies should guide or control "primitive" ones.

In short, blindness toward other cultures is produced by the conviction that opinions have objective foundations, the parochial nature of feelings, the tendency to turn superficial differences into hierarchies, and the drive for material wealth. As a result, common action becomes impossible, and the divisions within a society that should be mediated or resolved politically become fierce. The questions then arise, What should be the grounding for mutual respect? What kind of society would induce people to overcome their blindness, seek commonality with their fellow citizens, and tolerate the citizens of other countries?

James's proposals for overcoming blindness are implied in his analysis of its origins. In order to appreciate others' lives and values we must become less materialistic, and in political struggles we must abandon the stance that our side has a monopoly on truth.[53] Above all, we should acknowledge the formidable barriers to developing compassion for others, especially those much different than ourselves. It is too easy for the poor and working classes to see only the selfishness and softness of the bourgeoisie, and all too likely that the American Brahmins will find nothing to admire in workers and poor people. Gazing from a train at workmen building a bridge, James had a democratic vision:

> As I awoke to all this unidealized heroic life around me, the scales seemed to fall from my eyes; and a wave of sympathy greater than anything I have ever before felt with the common life of common men began to fill my soul. . . . In God's eyes the differences of social position, of intellect, of culture, of cleanliness, of dress, which different men exhibit, and all the other rarities and exceptions on which they so fantastically pin their pride, must be so small as practically quite to vanish. . . . [Each person has difficulties to overcome.] The exercise of courage, patience, and kindness, must be the significant portion of the whole business. . . . [Whenever we think that distinctions mean too much] some new leveller in the shape of a religious prophet has to arise—the Buddha, the Christ . . . some Rousseau or Tolstoi—to redispel our blindness. Yet, little by little, there comes some stable gain; for the world does get more humane, and the religion of democracy tends toward permanent increase.[54]

James himself attempted to be a democratic prophet and dispel the blindness that contributed to violence at home and imperialism abroad.

He argued in his essay "A Certain Blindness" that the people who care about something see its true value, and in making a judgment about it, the indifferent ones should defer to those who care.

> The spectator's judgment is sure to miss the root of the matter and to possess no truth. The subject judged knows a part of the world of reality which the judging spectator fails to see, knows more whilst the spectator knows less; and wherever there is a conflict of opinion and difference of vision, we are bound to believe that the truer side is the side that feels the more and not the side that feels the less.[55]

The one with experience and care knows more. To explain this point, James employed an analogy from personal life, writing that a particular person may appear drab to everyone else, but to the one in love with them their strengths are revealed.[56]

Surely poor Jill's palpitating little life-throbs *are* among the wonders of creation, *are* worthy of this sympathetic interest; and it is to our shame that the rest of us cannot feel like Jack. For Jack realizes Jill concretely, and we do not. [Jill responds to being known, however imperfectly, by seeing the best in Jack.] May the ancient blindness never wrap its clouds about either of them. . . . We ought, all of us, to realize each other in this intense, pathetic, and important way. . . . The vice of the ordinary Jack and Jill affection is not its intensity, but its exclusions and its jealousies. Leave those out, and you see that the ideal I am holding up before you, however impracticable to-day, yet contains nothing intrinsically absurd.[57]

James was not proposing that romantic love should become the model for political relationships—it is impossible to care intensely about everyone—but that we should recognize the psychological barriers to appreciating other people fully.[58] Admitting how difficult it is to value outlooks and ways of life different from our own might take some steam out of conflict. For James, mutual respect results from egalitarianism, rejection of materialism, obedience to the law, and self-doubt. Turning from James's framework, there are alternative paths toward mutual respect.

# IV

The topic of tolerance has become a major preoccupation of political theorists under such headings as "democracy and diversity," "multiculturalism," and "postmodernism and fundamentalism." Political theorists are doing their job by scrutinizing this critical issue in an era characterized by a breakdown of shared viewpoints and a rise of absolutist and fundamentalist movements. Questions of unity and disorder have been critical issues in the United States since the Puritans, and these issues became acute during the constitutional era and at the time of the Civil War. James's theory of mutual respect is in a tradition of which Abraham Lincoln was an important founder and in which sociologist Mary Parker Follett and political theorist John Schaar have been significant practitioners. Like them, William Connolly, a contemporary theorist deeply engaged with postmodernism, wants to create a democratic society in which citizens are sufficiently unified to act politically without suppressing local and individual differences. Connolly is, however, critical of the communitarian elements of radical democracy.

Connolly dispenses with state and national principles as a source of unity and draws on Nietzsche and Foucault in developing a position that is in some respects similar to that of James. They both see abandoning the claim to possess absolute truth as an important way to diminish antagonisms, and like James, Connolly designates such claims as a major source of domestic and international intolerance.[59] The formation of a personal or national identity is inevitable, but inherently dangerous; to adopt an identity requires labeling those unlike oneself as "others."[60] To illustrate Connolly's argument, I offer the following examples: Jews need the goyim (non-Jews) to help demarcate Judaism; Jews are the ones who do not drink milk with meat and do not work on the Sabbath. An expositor of Jewish customs explains:

> It should . . . be noted that Jewish conduct has always been greatly influenced by the practices of the outside world, particularly the Gentile world. For example, the Talmud . . . suggests that Jews in mourning not wear black shoes because this was a distinctly Gentile practice. What prompted Jews to require the wearing of a headcovering at religious services was an aversion to the Christian practice of keeping heads uncovered during worship.[61]

An important part of both black and white self-definition is knowing that each is not the other.[62] The majority culture typically needs the minority in order to feel the simultaneous movements of connection among themselves and exclusion of outsiders. Differences easily slide into hostility. "I have become a highly disciplined student, unlike those lazy good-for-nothings who sit in the back of the class." And one still hears statements like, "As an American, I am a citizen of the greatest country on earth; foreigners lack American freedom, democracy, wealth, and opportunity." Such proclamations justifiably annoy citizens of other countries who trust in their own country's virtues.

Because defining oneself against those who are different is an inherent part of identity formation, simply preaching tolerance as James did will have little effect. According to Connolly, efforts to create a unified community, nation, or international order will strengthen a hegemonic identity that suppresses resistant elements, classifying them as deviant. Instead of unity, Connolly advocates, in a Jamesian spirit, learning to value ambiguity, difference, and conflict in an "adversarial" democracy. The usual relationships among those who disagree are "conquest, conversion, community, or tolerance," but Connolly imagines a more dynamic possibility:

> Sometimes one shows respect for another by confronting him with alternative interpretations of himself, sometimes by just letting him be, sometimes by pursuing latent possibilities of commonality, sometimes by respecting her as the indispensable adversary whose contending identity gives definition to contingencies in one's own way of being.[63]

Connolly puts his ideal another way: to negotiate differences with others is "to convert an antagonism of identity into an agonism of difference in which each opposes the other (and the other's presumptive doctrines) while respecting the adversary at another level as one whose contingent orientations also rest on shaky epistemic grounds."[64] In other words, instead of fearing difference as if it were a disease and trying to cure it, antagonists should learn to welcome and even enjoy it. The premises of "agonistic" respect are twofold: first, one does not presume that one's position is grounded in absolute truth, and second, one acknowledges the necessity of opposition in creating identity and therefore is grateful to one's opponents for one's individuality.

Even after conceding that contestation over identity is an inherent element of political struggle, it is difficult to imagine political relationships forged by gratitude for alternative interpretations of oneself.[65] As president, Richard Nixon pictured himself as the country's protector from enemies foreign and domestic, but Senators Sam Ervin and George McGovern and thousands of antiwar protestors presented Nixon with a much different description of his identity, for which he never seemed particularly thankful. Civil rights activists give white supremacists and liberals accounts of their actions other than the ones they give themselves: segregationists are racists, not upholders of democratic localism; moderates and gradualists are identified as part of the problem. When Vietnam War protesters, who felt like patriots and highly moral friends-of-humanity, were called Communist dupes and traitors, they found such accusations surprising and painful. Connolly warns that discovering ambiguities in oneself is in itself insufficient grounds for generous action, because sometimes awareness of those ambiguities creates a discomfort and an anxiety that lead to violence. For example, the homophobe who discovers he is attracted to other men might strike out against gays.[66]

In what sense is a conflict of identities generous or amicable? When the foe of abortion accuses a woman who is terminating her pregnancy of being a "murderer," that is an adversarial but not a respectful interpretation of the woman's identity. Connolly might counter that the very process of rebutting an adversary's mislabeling is part of the identity formation for which one should be grateful. He illuminates a little-noticed element of political psychology, but his appealing suggestion to base generous relationships on gratitude for identity definition seems impossible to realize.

Like Connolly, John Schaar rejects some forms of unity as abstract, artificial, and dangerous. Schaar's enemy is nationalism, yet he endorses the national covenant as formulated by Lincoln as the best framework for mutual respect, community, and democratic participation. In Schaar's vision,

> Americans, a motley gathering of various races and cultures, were bonded together not by blood or religion, not by tradition or territory, not by the walls and traditions of a city, but by a political idea. We are a nation formed by a covenant, by dedication to a set of principles and by an exchange of promises to uphold and advance certain commitments among ourselves and throughout the world. Those principles and commitments are the core of American identity, the soul of the body politic.[67]

Lincoln and Schaar both designate the Declaration of Independence as the source of common principles, and, again paraphrasing Lincoln, Schaar exhorts his fellow citizens to

> see as the chief task of political life the task of political education: inculcate respect for valid laws as a "political religion": retell on every possible occasion the story of the struggle; teach tirelessly the principles of the founding. The only guardian of the compact is an informed citi-

zenry, and the first task of leadership is the formation of such a citizenry.[68]

Schaar softens Lincoln a little, implying that only "valid" laws should be respected. When he recommends that the founding principles should be "taught tirelessly," he means "considered both appreciatively and critically." Although he repudiates nationalism, a national covenant necessarily excludes the people who do not subscribe to its principles. What is the membership status of those not committed to individual rights, independence, and equality of opportunity? Presumably political theorists, whose work it is to examine reigning values, would find it difficult to remain loyal members of a society if they did not subscribe to its covenant.[69]

As Schaar explains, Lincoln sought unity among the multiple cultures and creeds of the citizens of the United States by asking for their commitment to national principles and obedience to the laws. If disagreements erupt into violent conflicts, both the "lawless in spirit" and their victims will disrespect the government.[70] To safeguard against revolution, Lincoln entreated:

Let every American, every lover of liberty . . . swear by the blood of the Revolution, never to violate in the least particular, the laws of the country; and never to tolerate their violation by others. . . . Let reverence for the laws, be breathed by every American mother, to the lisping babe, that prattles on her lap—let it be taught in schools, in seminaries; and in colleges;—let it be written in Primmers, spelling books, and in Almanacs;—let it be preached from the pulpit, proclaimed in the legislative halls, and enforced in courts of justice. And, in short, let it become the *political religion* of the nation; and let the old and young, the rich and poor, the grave and the gay, of all sexes and tongues, and colors and conditions, sacrifice unceasingly upon its altars.[71]

Lincoln's covenant is problematic because first, like Schaar's, it seeks to establish a national identity; second, unlike Schaar's, it prohibits civil disobedience; and third, the strong state that will promulgate laws and promote their acceptance may spread passivity among the citizens.[72] Schaar embraces Lincoln's formula because it overcomes "parochialisms of race and religion, and . . . severs patriotic devotion from the cult of national power."[73] This interpretation may be wishful thinking: it could be argued that Lincoln helped create the cult of centralized power by giving, partly through the concept of a national covenant, a religious fervor to American nationalism and by serving as its highly attractive symbol.[74] Could unity be nurtured among diverse and participatory American communities without inculcating national principles; might it emerge instead from a cross-cultural dialogue, a dialogue established on the critical study of one's community, other communities, and national history and political ideas?

One traditional path to mutual respect was explicitly rejected by the Federalists and revived by Tocqueville, Follett, and Arendt: political participation in community. Whereas the Federalists linked action with contentiousness, a more democratic tradition has viewed participation as the simultaneous creation of a common life and the self-conscious appreciation of it.[75] The initial motivation for becoming involved might be self-interest—people want their road repaired or their group to get a tax break—but through sustained interaction with their opponents they may come to appreciate them more and even value the democratic process itself.[76] For this transformation to occur, the political contact must be face-to-face. Genuine dialogue creates common ground in what Follett called a "subtle process of the intermingling of all the different ideas of the group." We come to see our connection with one another by putting forward our own ideas and being open to those of others. "Unity, not uniformity, must be our aim," she counseled. "We attain unity only through variety. Differences must be integrated, not annihilated, nor absorbed."[77]

To summarize the different viewpoints of a statesman, a philosopher, a sociologist of the early twentieth century, and of a late-twentieth-century political theorist, all want to preserve popular action, unity, and diversity and affirm love for one's own country and respect for other countries. Lincoln and James asserted that the institutions created by the Constitution are necessary to attain that balance; both advocated reverence for the laws as a central element in unity. Another approach to mutual respect, enunciated by Lincoln and Schaar, is founded on the inculcation of a national covenant and a common set of values contained in the Declaration of Independence. This covenant would be imparted through public exhortation or, less coercively, in Schaar's version, through the critical study of national history and political thought combined with an examination of other cultures, local and international. Connolly offers a different path to amiable relations among democratic citizens; he wishes they would result from a recognition that people unlike ourselves shape our identities. Finally, James, Follett, and Schaar thought of political participation as creating a foundation for mutual respect, and each of these theorists offers insight into the causes of cultural discord and the directions for overcoming it. A mixture of face-to-face political participation; humility about one's own righteousness combined with hesitance to condemn others; and the study of national, international, and local cultures seem to be three appealing, noncoercive paths toward mutual respect.

# V

I anticipate objections. Some readers will label James a "relativist" who might aid and abet such groups as Nazis, either by sanctioning their dogmas as being equal to anyone else's or by fostering appeasement. This charge would reveal a complete misinterpretation of James's position. He may have been generous in surmising that most people grasp part of the truth, but he was no fanatic. He recognized the existence of evil and thought that it should be combated, but he cautioned that sometimes we demonize those who disagree with us.

The Enlightenment promised that reason could unearth a truth that would be clear to all rational people, but James argued that reason offers no sure path to truth. Reason cannot disclose universal, unquestionable principles of right. Most people choose causes congruent with their personalities, so at best, reason may help us establish consistent principles and judge the consequences of our actions. Most of us act on faith mediated by some thinking and a modicum of evidence. Although we might not be able to prove it to an resolute opponent, we know that we are right about who should win an election or what to do about poverty, the death penalty, or nuclear testing. Our opponents are either deluded or people of bad intentions, yet they are as adamant as we are. A feeling of certainty cannot be the measure of truth.

James never denied the existence of truth and falsehood; the problem is that you can never be sure that you know the truth so you take a risk when you act according to your convictions. Like Hegel's owl of Minerva, which flies only at dusk, we are not sure until long afterward whether we did the right thing. Coming close to Socrates' notion of a "knowledge of ignorance" in "The Apology," James implied that we have some inkling of the truth, so that even if we lack certainty, we are not completely in the dark.

In addition, James stipulated that only "harmless" pleasures, a difficult term to define, should be tolerated. When genuine harm is done, intervention may be necessary. Mutual respect does imply the end of judgments about other cultures. When we perceive injury occurring in other countries, for example, in Haiti or Bosnia, any action we may need to take should be rooted in knowledge of that culture, including the existing diversity of positions.[78] We also need to remain aware, however, of our tendency to blindness.

James's theory of blindness and respect can also be criticized for being politically naive. He concentrated so much on the psychology of intolerance that he neglected institutions, power, ideology, and interests as causes of hostility.[79] For example, Marxists have contended that racism is not innate but has been fomented to divide working and poor people and to justify imperialism. Class interest, not psychology, is at the heart of social conflict, and James neglected the intuition of Rousseau in *The Social Contract* that a society cannot find commonality unless there is at least an approximate equality of wealth.[80] Without equality, conflicting groups will not see themselves as members of one society, and self-interest will then fuel hatred and make respect impossible.

Psychology is not more fundamental than power and interest in causing social conflict, but James illuminated the psychological dimension of conflict. To the assertion that the crucial problem to be addressed is not intolerance but injustice, James might have replied that he did not profess that pragmatism would create justice or end social strife but he did anticipate that a widespread adoption of the pragmatic outlook would reduce hatred so that conflicts could be resolved more peacefully. It may be that social harmony is impossible without the creation of just institutions and practices; such a hypothesis requires that a standard of justice be agreed upon and that a society would willingly be shaped according to it. How can that standard be determined? Whose interpretation of justice would be given institutional form? James clarified why such questions are difficult to resolve from the psychological standpoint and delineated the spirit needed to achieve their resolution. He may have added little to the analysis of the institutional dimension of the problem, but he contributed to the comprehension of the psychology of conflict and mutual respect.

The materialist critique of James cannot be easily dismissed and raises the broader issue of the practical effects of normative political theory. Theorists can argue for respect, direct democracy, or ideal speech communication, but who is listening? Theorists may suspect that in putting forth their alternative visions they are only giving solace to themselves and a few sympathetic readers.[81] The people who need to hear the argument for respect will not listen to it—if the Bosnian Serbs had read either James or a critique of nationalism such as Benedict Anderson's *Imagined Communities,* would they have stopped the killing?[82]

Can the rhetoric of toleration, coming from academic, political, or religious sources, appeal to a large audience? It can sound clichéd or utopian and perhaps will reach only the people who subscribe to it already. The language of hatred, on the other hand—the language of Louis Farrakhan or Ariel Sharon—always sounds tough-minded; it may be appalling, but it wins new followers. Is the discourse of equality and respect—from Jesus to Tolstoy, Locke to Mill, Gandhi to King—all superstructure, or has it had an influence in restraining violence and hatred? Evidence could be mustered that nonviolent, democratic visions have had an effect as they have helped lead the way to the civil rights and feminist movements.

A second dimension of the question concerning the power of political visions is more specific to academic political theory. Although every theorist dreams of advising fellow citizens and even readers abroad, the reality is that comparatively few people read scholarly books and any one teacher reaches only a handful of citizens in college classrooms. On the other hand, a lot of people go to school, and from universities to grammar schools, American education has been altered by challenges to the Western canon, new attention to anthropology, non-Western history, women's history, gay and lesbian studies, radical democratic thought, feminist and postmodern philosophies. These educational innovations can be seen as a democratic "correction" of the sort that James attributed to Christ, Rousseau, and Tolstoy.

Recent movements for civil rights, feminism, radical democracy, and equal rights for gays and for the handicapped might be seen as democratic efforts to overcome an "ancestral blindness" that prevent us from recognizing the contributions of previously disrespected groups. Yet I recognize that we seem to be entering a period of a sweeping reaction against equality, and James's faith that "little by little, there comes some stable gain; for the world does get more humane, and the religion of democracy tends toward permanent increase" appears to be more solace than an accurate prediction of the near future. The anti-equality movements also have their theorists opposing affirmative action and equal rights for gays and lesbians, and some of those theorists are fundamentalists who reject democratic debate as moral weakness. One hopes that both sides adopt a tincture of Jamesian mutual respect so that the struggle can proceed nonviolently.

## Chapter 4
# Faith and Doubt: Action's Wellsprings

James wanted to cultivate in Americans both action and mutual respect, and he developed a model of a democratic political temperament that would hold them together. He urged citizens to adopt the pluralist conception of truth, i.e., political actors should seek to fulfill their ideals without taking those ideals to be objectively or absolutely true. If people will accept the fact that they alone are responsible for their fates, then they must strive together to create the conditions they desire. And in recognizing that truths and institutions are human choices, people are less likely to embrace their ideals zealously.[1] This process of creating a democratic temperament requires both demystification and the strength to persevere in taking action. "The pragmatism or pluralism which I defend has to fall back on a certain ultimate hardihood, a certain willingness to live without assurances or guarantees."[2]

In *Pragmatism*, James asserted, exaggeratedly, that demystification had already been accomplished in politics and religion and now needed to be adopted by philosophy. "In other spheres of life it is true that we have got used to living in a state of relative insecurity. The authority of 'the State' and that of an absolute 'moral law,' have resolved themselves into expediencies, and holy church has resolved itself into 'meeting houses.' "[3] Elsewhere, James suggested that uncertainty had not been widely embraced. In order to respect others, fervent political actors should acquire some doubt about their convictions while realizing that even their opponents possess a share of the truth.[4] The joining of committed action with comprehension of the opposition is appealing and even necessary for direct democracy, but James disguised the psychological difficulty of keeping them together.

Although James offered pluralism as a source of both action and respect, the psychological roots of the one are incompatible with the other. He understood that action usually springs from a passionate belief in a principle and that this passionate belief leads the typical political actor to

81

resist pluralism. Most political actors will neither doubt the truth of their positions nor deeply respect their opponents, and if they did, they might cease to act. According to Wolin: "Under present circumstances, any kind of recognition of the other person's point of view is seen as ammunition by political consultants for labeling opponents as wafflers. James's analysis shows—even though he did not intend it—some of the practices we've slipped into in recent years that make political dialogue very difficult."[5]

Dismissing James at this point for being "unrealistic" in his call for mutual respect may be based on a static conception of political action. Perhaps, as Mary Parker Follett suggested, the process of interpersonal political interaction under certain conditions can produce a sympathetic understanding between engaged adversaries. "It is possible to maintain that at one point the civil rights movement had the effect of leading southerners to understand the black position," suggests Wolin, "or at least their own treatment of blacks in a somewhat different light. It is hard to say what we have now."[6] A second avenue toward mutual respect offered by pragmatism must also be explored: Will pragmatism's refocusing of political discussions from principles to consequences reduce hostility?

# I

As James examined the prospects for American democracy at the end of the nineteenth century, he saw two equally problematic groups of citizens who constituted politically relevant audiences for his pluralist theory: one that acts on faith and another paralyzed because its members lack faith.

> Of course if any one comes along and says that men at large don't need to have facility of faith in their inner convictions preached to them, [that] they have only too much readiness in that way already, and the one thing needful to preach is that they should hesitate with their convictions, and take their faiths out for an airing into the howling wilderness of nature, I should also agree. But my paper ["The Will to Believe"] was n't addressed to mankind at large but to a limited set of studious persons, badly under the ban just now of certain authorities

whose simple-minded faith in "naturalism" also is sorely in need of an airing—and an airing, as it seems to me, of the sort I tried to give.[7]

The first, and larger, group engaged in action based on unquestioned faith. They had admirable, public-minded energy but tended toward fanatic violence and imperialism. The second group, "studious persons," had withdrawn into private life because they had lost faith in a God who cared about human affairs, including politics in the United States. What good is action if it is not guided or assured by God or some other principle of meaning, such as Hegel's absolute spirit or Marx's theory of history? The classic articulation of this despair is Henry Adams's *Education*.[8] As a path out of resignation and toward democratic action, James offered the pluralist explanation of the universe to both believers and skeptics. Pluralism would allow the doubters to act based on choice in place of their lost faith; it would also reduce the fervor of the citizens who continue to act upon faith.

What view of truth did James offer to these groups? To put it briefly, he imagined a "pluralist universe" in which no higher power determines human fate, in which beliefs are chosen rather than discovered or proved and cultures and institutions are construed as human constructions.[9] "Laws and languages . . . are thus seen to be man-made things."[10] According to James, God has not written a discernible text of commandments for humanity to obey; truth exists, but it cannot be clearly apprehended. Therefore, people create social realities by acting upon their best guesses as to what the good actually is. These guesses should be based on reason, study, knowledge of accepted truths, customs, personality, and, finally, faith.[11] Truth functions in moral, religious, and political life as a hypothesis. We do not know if we are members of the true church, but our church will thrive only if we believe in it.[12]

People who act must be reconciled to the possibility of failure. Some initiatives for new parties, organizations, institutions, vocabulary, and theories are successful, but most, whatever good they might do for those who participate and witness them, fail to become permanent or achieve their goals.[13] Would-be founders take two kinds of risks. First, despite their best intentions, their aims and tactics may be misguided—e.g., by running a third-party candidate the lesser of two evils lost the election; when protestors did not compromise, government hard-liners got the upper hand. Second, sometimes advocates of the most moral cause simply lack the means to succeed. Action has no guarantees. James surmised that this view of truth would give something important to both believers and skeptics. Embracing uncertainty would, he hoped, make citizens more energetic and political partisans more generous toward their opponents.

## II

I would like now to elaborate the effects that James intended for pluralism to have on his two different audiences. He wanted them to come to the democratic temperament from two different directions. James did not consistently believe that we are motivated to act by the idea of a pluralist universe; by nature, he often said, we are inclined the other way, i.e., we need faith in the grounding of our ideals. Perry remarked, "For James life assumes a heroic form only when the moral subject believes in the superiority of his own ideal, not as merely his, but as in some sense absolute or infinite."[14] James wrote that the political actor is like the Christian saint in that both are moved by a truth that they take to be greater than themselves. The saint has

> a feeling of being in a wider life than that of this world's selfish interests; and a conviction, not merely intellectual, but as it were sensible, of the existence of an Ideal power. In Christian saintliness this power is always personified as God; but abstract moral ideals, civic or patriotic utopias, or inner visions of holiness or right may also be felt as the true lords and enlargers of our life.

The saint's energy and, one can infer by analogy, the energy of committed political actors come in large part from their "sense of the friendly continuity of the ideal power with our own life, and a willing self-surrender to its control."[15]

James's description of the saint captures a fundamental strain of the American political tradition. He could have been speaking about Jefferson, Paine, Hamilton, or William Lloyd Garrison when he wrote, "Political reformers accomplish their successive tasks in the history of nations by being blind for the time to other causes."[16] This way of thinking may not be peculiarly American, but it is an American tradition to believe that when we act, God is on our side.[17] The Puritans saw New England as a light for the entire world, and American revolutionaries and the constitutional framers similarly posited a unique historical role for U.S. political principles and practices.

When individuals claim that their rights are being violated, they tend to echo Jefferson's formulation, "We hold these truths to be self-evident, that all men are created equal, that they are endowed by their creator with certain inalienable rights."[18] "It has been frequently remarked," wrote Alexander Hamilton in the first number of The Federalist, "that it seems to have been reserved to the people of this country, by their conduct and example, to decide the important question, whether societies of men are really capable or not of establishing good government from reflection and choice, or whether they are forever destined to depend for their political constitutions on accident and force."[19] If the United States failed, given its highly favorable circumstances and ability to make a fresh start, then no country could establish a free government. Most subsequent steps in American history, including the civil rights movement, have sought to link God, country, and cause. For example, many of the people who supported the war in Vietnam believed that the United States embodied good while the North Vietnamese were evil incarnate. James's critique could also be applied to the Christian right and the anti-Communist crusade that depicted the Soviet Union as the evil empire.

Although James respected, for the good it produced, the American tradition of action based on faith, he wanted to transform that tradition in order to reduce the imperialist impulse and to make political resolution of differences possible. Mutual respect will be fostered if people with excessive zeal, a group that includes ordinary citizens as well as political activists, accept the pluralist model of the universe. The fervent ones need to learn hesitation and doubt so they will toil for their causes without claiming to possess all virtue. A tincture of self-doubt makes democratic respect feasible. Perry summarized James's position:

The grip of the hand on the sword is relaxed by the reflection that the other's cause is as real and warm to him as is mine to me, and has its own inner and equal justification. If the principle of sympathy be given priority over the principle of self-assertion it is still possible, however, to save the militant and heroic qualities. The principle of sympathy is itself a cause for moral and even for physical courage.[20]

James's description of typical political action based on fervent belief in one's convictions contrasts sharply with the pluralist model he proposed. Without ever saying so explicitly, he appears to have been calling for a transformation of the traditional American political consciousness. Wolin augments this argument: "If you ask, what does the person of faith, the devout person, have to give up in order to embrace a pluralist universe, the answer is 'quite a bit.' James is demanding a great deal that would involve, one might argue, a radical change of character. He or she would cease to be a fervent believer."[21] From James's characterization of committed actors in *Varieties of Religious Experience*, there seems to be little grounds for success in effecting this metamorphosis, even though he proposed pragmatism as an alternative at the end of that book. Would he have had a better chance of altering the outlook of his second audience, those who lack faith?

# III

In addition to the people who have excessive certainty, James spoke to those who fear there is no solid ground for taking action, a paralyzing doubt that has recently assumed different forms. In the sixties and seventies, many people said they could not engage in politics "until they got their heads together." In part, this was a statement of priorities, but it also identified "the head" as the filter of values, visions, programs, and actions; if the head were "not together," a person might make destructive choices and act inefficiently. I remain friends with a woman who entered a would-be revolutionary party, a cult really, instead of finishing college. Upon her escape from it, under threat to her life, she became disillusioned with all politics because she does not know whom to trust. After Watergate, Vietnam, the Soviet Union, the Cultural Revolution, and Tiananmen Square, what will replace unquestioning conviction as an inspiration for action?

James asked the same question in response to a much different set of events. In the nineteenth century, the carnage of the Civil War, the corruption of the second Grant administration, and the Darwinian revolution were interpreted as indicators of the universe's absence of meaning.[22] As a young man, James himself experienced a loss of faith and suffered a nervous breakdown, recovering only after reading the work of the philosopher Charles Renouvier, who posited that principles could be freely chosen instead of scientifically discovered.[23] James addressed his essay "The Will to Believe" to people who feared they could not act meaningfully in a random and chaotic universe. He prescribed to American skeptics the cure that had worked for him: beliefs grounded in choice rather than ontology and the fact that ideals need not be based on external, objective foundations.

> For pluralistic pragmatism, truth grows up inside of all the finite experiences. They lean on each other, but the whole of them, if such a whole there be, leans on nothing. All "homes" are in finite experience; finite experience as such is homeless. Nothing outside of the flux secures the issue of it. It can hope salvation only from its own intrinsic promises and potencies.[24]

James's response to this lack of certainty became, Believe in what you need. When asked in an interview whether he believed in God, he said yes, because he needed Him. Of course, James's assertion can be made to seem absurd—I need a glass of water so I believe it is there—but James's proposition is actually close to everyday experience. Is the job worth doing? For example, is it worthwhile to write books or attempt to teach young people in a "postliterate" age? Should time be spent in dingy offices making fliers for rallies that will draw only a handful of people? We can and should advance evidence and arguments in favor of our positions, but we cannot prove that our activities matter. Yet, in order to stick with them, we need to believe that they do.[25]

James hoped that adopting this outlook would not only help skeptics overcome paralysis but make their eventual actions less belligerent. He was arguing not simply for a recovery of traditional American faith but for a redefinition of faith to incorporate self-conscious doubt. Faith, he wrote, is "belief in something concerning which doubt is still theoretically possible." This new understanding would be accepted, James thought, because people would rise to a challenge. "Any mode of conceiving the universe which . . . makes the man seem as if he were individually helping to create the actuality of the truth whose metaphysical reality he is willing to assume, will be sure to be responded to by large numbers."[26]

I have shown that James offered the pluralist universe to two types of political actors. He invited the faithful to a measure of doubt and skeptics to generous action based upon new guiding principles. Ideals would remain the inspiration for action, but the political actors would not assume those ideals to be guaranteed by anything other than choice. Having described James's pluralism as one element of a democratic political temperament, I now want to turn to another tool he offered democratic citizens, pragmatism.

## IV

In everyday language, pragmatism implies the practical and the concrete. In politics, the call to "be pragmatic" means to settle for what you can get. Its opposite is rigid idealism or an insistence upon inopportune discussion of principles when the situation demands action. These definitions are only indirectly related to James's position, which proffers pragmatism as both a theory of truth and a method of resolving fierce philosophical and political conflicts. His concerns intersect with everyday language at one point, however: to take a "pragmatic" view of truth in political discussions is to consider the consequences of a proposed idea rather than dispute first principles.

Instead of posing such dilemmas as, What is justice? or Should a society guarantee equality of condition or only equality of opportunity? political opponents should imagine the potential results of implementing their respective principles. James would try to redirect a political conversation toward the query, If we accept your view to be true rather than mine, what difference does it make to our course of action?[27] Where there is no difference in result, James posited, there is no meaningful difference in principles. James thought that disputes often could be resolved by showing that if either position were implemented the effects would be the same. In politics, policy debates usually create different repercussions; where they do not, James is right, the debate can cease. But once anticipated effects are established, political opponents must assess them, which leads back to fundamental principles.

One might assume that pragmatism is the enemy of political theory because it disparages an overlong consideration of ideals. Machiavelli was an ancestor of political pragmatism, given this definition of it: in politics power, context, and consequences must always be considered. "A great many men have imagined states and princedoms such as nobody ever saw or knew in the real world, for there's such a difference between the way we really live and the way we ought to live that the man who neglects the real to study the ideal will learn how to accomplish his ruin, not his salvation."[28] The just person who goes into the world unarmed will be ineffectual. Machiavelli never denied the existence of justice and truth, and never suggested that might makes right, but he had no faith that right makes might.

Political theory's stock-in-trade is debate of first principles, and so it will always be an enemy of vulgar pragmatism, but this fact does not foreclose consideration of the narrower issue of turning to consequences as a method for reducing the intensity of political conflict. As a rhetorical strategy, James's proposal is attractive, but it is unlikely to be effective because there is no clear distinction between first principles and consequences. It would be splendid if turning to outcomes reduced terrorism:

> The national government is indeed dangerous, but if you bomb either the plane or the building many innocent people will be hurt.
> Really? Then forget the whole thing.

Civilian deaths are not assessed uniformly. Some people believe that no lives of the enemy are "innocent." Deaths are unfortunate, but necessary to gain attention for the cause. People are dying all the time at the hands of military force, and some lives must be sacrificed in order to stop injustice. This view might remind some readers of Machiavelli's insight that a discussion of repercussions requires as much imagination as does a debate about principles because in politics, and even in life, no one knows what the actual effects of an action will be. Anticipated consequences are often ironically related to intentions.

It might be countered that examining consequences rather than debating first principles would reduce emotions and make resolution more likely, but it is remarkable how little impact pragmatic arguments have on those people who assert that only morality matters. In the abortion debate, one might say, "Let us not focus solely on the question of when life begins and whether all human life must be protected but instead remember that the outcomes of making abortions illegal would be that only wealthy women could afford them while other women would have more unwanted children and many women would seek dangerous illegal abortions." Some Catholics among others argue that the most serious consequences of free choice on abortion will be a callousness about life and an avoidance of personal responsibility, and one cannot convince an orthodox Catholic or Jew that abortion or birth control is necessary to prevent the consequence of overpopulation. Flannery O'Connor wrote in a letter:

> The Church's stand on birth control is the most absolutely spiritual of all her stands and with all of us being materialists at heart, there is little wonder that it causes unease. I wish various fathers would quit trying to defend it by saying that the world can support 40 billion. I will rejoice in the day when they say: This is right, whether we all rot on top of each other or not, dear children, as we certainly may. Either practice restraint or be prepared for crowding.[29]

I do not accept O'Connor's view, but it reveals that even if effects should be considered in assessing the validity of a proposed action, it is unlikely that political actors motivated by faith will be willing to shift consideration from first principles to consequences or that they would weigh those consequences similarly. To suggest that someone shift from a consideration of principles to consequences is really to ask them to change their identity.

## V

James sought to inspire both citizen action and mutual respect with his conception of a pluralist universe in which beliefs are grounded in choice rather than in something external. Would this vision be compelling enough to inspire skeptics to act? Would it soften the hard edges of those driven by faith without discouraging them altogether? James himself supposed that great political action was usually fueled by deep faith. Even if activists have never heard of debates about epistemology, they tend to hold to their beliefs tenaciously, acting as if those beliefs were objectively true. The cultivation of doubt and tolerance might make political actors more generous but less impelled to act. Doubt may be an essential component of scholarship, but not of politics; fervent political actors are usually not skeptics. The rest of us may often recognize strong arguments on both sides of an issue, and be thankful that we do not have to decide, but partisans feel their cause to be righteous. Would the notion of a pluralist universe really motivate action if, as James posited, action typically emerges from faith in a cause? Can a freely chosen ideal, experienced as freely chosen, produce the same inspiration? His description of action inspired by faith seems truer to the experience of transformative political action; the proposed alternative, action based on choice and respect for others, is attractive but difficult to achieve.

As James conceded, confidence in the absolute virtue of one's aims has been a typical component of great political efforts. An intellectual biographer of Frederick Douglass writes:

> Without a spiritual anchor to rely upon, without a God of justice to overrule a society that promised only injustice, without the simple but powerful theory that history is a process where things somehow get better, and without a fierce commitment to agitation, black leaders could not realistically have continued to exhort their people to remain hopeful of a life and opportunity and dignity in the face of oppression.[30]

If James exhorted, "Believe in what you need," what were the psychological needs of Ida B. Wells who tried in the 1890s to stop lynching and attain the vote for women in the face of massive, often violent resistance, even from white suffragettes? Did she not need unquestioning conviction in the justice of her struggle?[31] Could Martin Luther King, Jr., who tried to love his enemies, have continued his work if he had not believed that racial equality was an unequivocal good? He wrote, "We will win our freedom because the sacred heritage of our nation and the eternal will of God are embodied in our echoing demands."[32] It is difficult to picture a pluralist, postmodern King who did not tie his crusade to heavenly will.[33]

Recognition of a pluralistic universe might give strength to some people in despair, but it could undermine the determination of committed activists. One can imagine a person who is afraid that nothing can be changed because everything is controlled by large forces—you can't fight city hall or progress, to say nothing of late capitalism—being able to find inspiration in the notions that those forces do not govern history, present conditions have not been sanctioned by God or the march of history, and people can, at least to a degree, affect the world in a meaningful way. But one can also envision activists who become discouraged if they adopt the vision of a pluralistic universe and conclude that their cause lacks objective superiority. In short, action and respect may have contradictory sources. What produces one undermines the other so that the natural tendency is toward either fanatic action or tolerant passivity. Are these the only alternatives?

The authors of The Federalist had a solution: since politics inflames the passions, they designed institutions to reduce political participation.[34] Although James may have supported the Constitution in principle, institutions and practices that promoted passivity were unacceptable to him, and thus he implicitly rejected the Federalist contempt for action. An inert populace is unlikely to be more tolerant than an active one, if only because political participants often learn about their opponents by working with them politically rather than fearing them as imaginary enemies. James demanded that the person of deep faith should continue to work for his or her causes but become more pluralistic upon entering the realm of politics. In effect, James was calling for a new type of political actor, yet he made it clear why that type will be difficult to create. The tension between faith and pluralism that can be seen in James's theory does not mean that the democratic temperament is impossible to engender, but it does mean that it will not be easy to do so. James's proposed combination of action and mutual respect should be judged to be, not so much a contradiction, as a formidable and worthy goal.

*Chapter 5*

# Democratic Teaching

For William James, the school was a crucial site for imparting the democratic temperament. James insisted that the welfare of the nation depends upon having thoughtful citizens who attempt to realize their ideas and ideals while respecting other citizens and cultures. Therefore, the ideas disseminated in the classroom should produce activity. For James, it would be insufficient for students to discuss conceptions of justice; they should then try to create just conditions in the world. Nevertheless, James's proposal for the distribution of knowledge at first appears to be quite elitist: his call for the creation of an aristocracy of the college educated might be heard as an appeal for a well-trained ruling class. In this chapter, I try to establish that the elitism of James's educational program is mitigated by its democratic function, preparing citizens for self-rule, and that democracy is not incompatible with elitism of a certain kind.

## I

Recently, the most prominent debates about the relationship between politics and education have emphasized the importance of the curriculum while neglecting a different aspect of politics and education, i.e., that of student character or personality. Yet this concern has been central to the tradition of political theory, especially in the works of Plato, Rousseau, Thoreau, Tocqueville, Weber, and Foucault. In the *Oxford English Dictionary* education and character are linked in one definition of "education": "culture or development of powers, formation of character, as contrasted with the imparting of mere knowledge or skill." The character of the good student is similar to that of the democratic citizen. True students and citizens are courageous, independent, and willing to engage others in spirited, but ultimately respectful dialogue about differences. These students and

93

citizens energetically respond to their world. The same spark that produces inquiry creates an inclination to action, which is common to both learning and democracy.

Spiritless students become passive citizens who cannot shoulder the burdens of governance. They are unable to seek the truth behind the manipulative rhetoric of politicians and advertisers, and they lack the energy and skill to analyze complexities of power and the nature of justice, much less engage in collective action. Passive students do not learn well. They let the words of the books pass before their eyes, and the lectures and class discussions float past their ears, but little except the discipline—the tests, grades, required attendance—penetrates to their souls, where real learning occurs. Many educational practices undermine democracy by promoting submissiveness in the students. From the perspective of the educator, passivity is disastrous, as widespread resignation indicates a tragic stifling of the human capacity for free action grounded in reason, passion, and commitment.

Some readers might feel uncomfortable with applying political categories to teaching because they believe the classroom should be independent of politics. Perhaps at the office or factory, workers might have to watch carefully what they say about politics or company policy—free speech is not protected on the job—but in the classroom and in writing, students should be free to disagree with each other, with the text, or with the professor so long as they accept rules of evidence, grammar, rhetorical argument, and civility. The classroom should indeed be a space for the free exchange of ideas, but a few moments' reflection reveals that education is neither power-free nor purely democratic.

Democracy aspires to equality of power, but power in the classroom and power in the institution are not equal. The legitimacy of the teachers' authority to give students grades or evaluations derives from the formers' superior command both of the subject and of the standards of academic excellence. The students also have strength: they can kill discussion through sullen silence, or by entering it they can enable even mediocre teachers to transmit their knowledge. Student evaluations give the students additional leverage, particularly over untenured faculty. Although many evaluations are filled out thoughtfully, some students use them as a form of revenge against professors. Many faculty members bitterly resent student evaluations, finding it humiliating to be criticized by young people, especially undergraduates, and their resentment may emanate, at least in part, from the power reversal. Such faculty members often are the most jealous of their privileges and power, and their contempt for students often surprises me: "No eighteen-year-old is going to tell me how or what to teach." By contrast, William James contended that if students were given more power in governing a university, they would begin to act more responsibly. (Although James did invite students to criticize his courses, today's student evaluations, which are usually written in haste and anonymously, tend not to embody this principle of responsibility.) James attempted to develop a theory of pedagogy in which power in the classroom would be used to foster the democratic temperament.

Democratic pedagogy does not imply equal power for teacher and student but, instead, the preparation of students for democratic citizenship. Ideally, the classroom is a place where students acquire the abilities to articulate their thoughts both orally and in writing, to scrutinize and appreciate traditional wisdom while being open to new and strange ideas, and obtaining the historical, linguistic, and theoretical knowledge needed to begin to comprehend their own and other cultures. Finally, the democratic classroom imparts to students a certain character (partly described in Chapter 2), which involves being intellectually independent, critical, courageous, imaginative, and respectful of others.

I fear that many of my students, admirable as they are in other ways, lack this democratic character. For the purpose of analysis I will describe an ideal type, in the Weberian sense, of student. As with all ideal types, many students do not fit it, yet I believe it captures part of the ethos of generation X. Many of today's students are curious but intellectually indolent. If a book, newspaper, or challenging film is not assigned, they will ignore it. They do not want to appear foolish or so concerned about matters intellectual or political that they seem depressed or weird. They are more comfortable in front of a screen—television, computer, or video game—than in front of a book. They have good intentions: they would stop pollution, war, prejudice, and rape; they want to feed the hungry and shelter the homeless. But they do not want to speak in class or in public, much less organize any sort of political action.[1] They are cynical about authorities but eager to please their parents, teachers, and each other.

They experience and accept the classroom as power-laden. Why must they attend class and arrive on time? If they come late or not at all, it's their loss, not the professor's. They read books they hate, attend classes that bore them, record and repeat on examinations lecture formulas that often make no sense to them. Papers must be submitted by arbitrary deadlines. Professors always win in a dispute about grades, even though the student knows more about how much was learned in the class than the teacher does. The students endure teachers who are cruel and sarcastic, sexist or politically correct in order to get the grade that is necessary for a good job or admission to some type of graduate school.[2] The questions, Is this what I really think? Is this what I really want to do? rarely arise.

Students often embody Karl Marx's description of alienated laborers.

What constitutes the alienation of labour? First, that the work is external to the worker, that it is not part of his nature; and that, consequently, he does not fulfill himself in his work but denies himself, has a feeling of misery rather than well-being, does not develop freely his mental and physical energies, but is physically exhausted and mentally debased. . . . His work is not voluntary but imposed, forced labour. It is not the satisfaction of a need, but only a means for satisfying other needs. Its alien character is clearly shown by the fact that as soon as there is no physical or other compulsion, it is avoided like the plague. . . . We arrive at the result that man (the worker) feels himself to be freely active only in his animal functions—eating, drinking, and procreating, or at most also in his dwelling and in personal adornment.[3]

Some college students cannot wait for weekends, which begin Thursday night, when they can get blind drunk and relieve the tension created by hypocrisy. Silent in the classroom, they are boisterous in the bar, at the rock concert, and on the playing field. Drawing on James's *Talks to Teachers* and his public letters on education, one could attribute the students' alienation to their feeling of powerlessness as students, citizens, and workers.[4]

Professors hate the silence of the students and their lack of initiative. We want them to care about their own learning—to do extra reading, not the minimum. We wish they would appear more eager about class. It is disheartening to watch students cheer when they see a sign posted that a professor is ill and must cancel class. Class periods often begin with some student faces covered with boredom, heads down on the desks, showing every sign of still suffering from a vicious hangover at two in the afternoon. During discussions, many appear unresponsive; they do not want to answer the teacher's questions and they ask none of their own. After years of paranoia, I have learned that blank looks may not indicate that students don't care: they may be interested, but they refuse to reveal it in their faces or in any other aspect of their behavior.

Student passivity and anti-intellectualism are built into the culture and into the structure of educational institutions, but what effect do professors have upon the students?[5] Do we contribute to student resignation or disrupt it? Using Foucault's language, we might ask, What disciplinary practices do professors exercise upon the students, and what type of character or subjects do we create through those disciplinary practices?[6] Have we encouraged their dependence on us for approval of their ideas? In correcting and reproving students, have we broken their will, made them feel stupid and incompetent to think or write clearly? Can the teacher's authority be used to undermine student apathy? If we are tired of the listlessness of young people today, the bored looks, the silence, how can we wake them up? I am not suggesting that classrooms or families be transformed into little Greek assemblies, but I would argue that in a democracy, professors and parents should use their authority to invigorate young people in the classroom and the world outside.

William James linked the active student with the citizen in his writings about education. These writings can be read politically by placing them in the context of his call for a dynamic body politic, his description of aggressive human instincts that require taming by reason, and his celebration of heroes and geniuses. James advocated a pedagogy that would encourage students to be responsive and strong-willed, but he was not entirely democratic in his thinking about the distribution of knowledge. He wanted the college-educated to serve as a leadership class to balance popular instincts, and he urged the people to act vigorously while being led and checked by an intellectual elite. Is this a contradiction, and if so, what is its meaning? Was James ambivalent about democracy, or is this type of educational elite actually, as he claimed it to be, consistent with democracy?

# II

James called for Americans to overcome paralysis by embracing action founded on chosen beliefs, and he developed an influential pedagogy compatible with democratic action. He applied his psychological theories explicitly and his political principles implicitly to the art of teaching in his influential text *Talks to Teachers on Psychology*, which was widely used in teacher training and reprinted twenty-three times between 1899 and 1929. He considered teaching to be his vocation, of both Harvard students and the American public, and he identified education as a crucial component in preserving American democracy.[7] James was an innovative teacher.[8] A famous story is told about Gertrude Stein who studied with James when she attended Radcliffe. After reading the questions on a final exam, Stein wrote a note, "Dear Professor James, I am so sorry but really I do not feel like an examination paper in philosophy today," and left the class. The next day she received James's reply: "Dear Miss Stein, I understand perfectly how you feel. I often feel like that myself." He gave her the highest mark in the class.[9] He enjoyed being challenged during lectures, and as a proto-Bakthinian, disliked delivering monologues.[10] He surprised his students by asking them at the end of his courses to assess them.

James's wish that citizens should be forceful, independent, and generous flowed from his pedagogical principles, and he sought to create in students a balance between action and thought. Teaching must be conducted in such a manner that the dynamic character of the students, who are naturally bold, curious, and energetic, will be maintained. He asserted that teachers should stimulate students' imaginations, inspire them, and discipline them without paralyzing their wills. "Although you have to generate in your pupils a large stock of ideas, any one of which may be inhibitory, yet you must also see to it that no habitual hesitancy or paralysis of the will ensues, and that the pupil still retains his power of vigorous action."[11]

James feared that elements of the intellectual life might induce paralysis: the universe could appear frighteningly complex; the habit of study induces rumination rather than reaction; one could become so balanced in outlook, so used to seeing all sides of the question, that one becomes unable to act. James declared, "Not to be able to proceed to extremities, to be still able to act energetically under an array of inhibitions—that indeed is rare and difficult."[12] Although some inhibitions are necessary—only a maniac behaves and speaks without inhibition while a "melancholiac is so inhibited that he does not act at all"—in the ideal citizen, action overcomes inhibitions.[13] James repudiated reckless, impulsive action without regard to consequences as dangerous, but the opposite and equal danger is no action at all. "There is no more contemptible type of human character than that of the nerveless sentimentalist and dreamer, who spends his life in a weltering sea of sensibility, but never does a concrete manly deed."[14]

Because education's primary purpose is not to transmit ideas or information, but to supply students with resources for action, James held that pupils should be encouraged to react to what they learn rather than memorizing and repeating it.[15] In order to create something other than submissive students, teachers should appeal to student interest, not fear. Reliance on coercion to gain the students' attention "is a wasteful method, bringing bad temper and nervous wear and tear as well as imperfect results. The teacher who can get along by keeping spontaneous interest excited must be regarded as the teacher with the greatest skill."[16] James also subscribed to "a complete system of self-government by the students." Students should be treated as adults and given responsibility for their own affairs.[17] He claimed that students at Harvard had become more mature in large part because of an "all but complete remission of paternalism in the Faculty-government." The way to improve the conduct of students is to give them more power.[18]

James exhorted colleges to impart to their students (and students to the rest of the society) a liberal temper, tightening up the minds of the romantics—making them clearer thinkers who establish evidence for their propositions—while "softening" those trained exclusively in the hard sciences—leading them to realize the importance of poetry, questioning, and imagination.[19] He desired that students be able to think vigorously and independently and hoped they would develop open, tolerant, and unconventional minds.[20] Knowing "the chief rival attitudes towards life," he wrote, is the "essential part of liberal education. Philosophy, indeed, in one sense of the term is only a compendious name for the spirit in education which the word 'college' stands for in America."[21] The students who imbibe this spirit of action and openness would serve as the teachers of the democratic citizenry, which leads to the question, What is the source of authority for democracy's teachers?

# III

If James's theory of pedagogy was democratic, his model for distributing knowledge was elitist. What is the meaning of this new Jamesian paradox? How was his elitism different from that of democracy's true enemies? Before trying to salvage James as a democrat, I will describe his vision of the educational elite, the function of that group, and the processes of creating it and spreading its influence.

The most antidemocratic element of James's educational theory was his sharp distinction between extraordinary leaders and the common people. As I showed in Chapter 1, James believed that communities determine their fate by following rare individuals.[22]

The notion that a people can run itself and its affairs anonymously is now well known to be the silliest of absurdities. Mankind does nothing save through initiatives on the part of inventors, great or small, and imitation by the rest of us—these are the sole factors active in human progress. Individuals of genius show the way, and set the patterns, which common people then adopt and follow.[23]

The world . . . is only beginning to see that the wealth of a nation consists more than in anything else in the number of superior men that it harbors. . . . Geniuses are ferments; and when they come together as they have done in certain lands at certain times, the whole population seems to share in the higher energy which they awaken.[24]

The distinction between "superior" and "ordinary" cannot be debated here, but it can be noted that the role of the "superior" ones is to awaken energy in "the whole population." Although it is true that James chose representative rather than direct democracy, he did not say that the people cannot govern themselves—after all, he called for student self-government—only that they cannot do so "anonymously," i.e., without leaders. He also argued, as Tocqueville did in *Democracy in America*, that democracies require an influential aristocratic component. "In our democracy, where everything else is so shifting," James wrote, "we alumni and alumnae of the colleges are the only permanent presence that corresponds to the aristocracy in older countries. . . . We stand for ideal interests solely, for we have no corporate selfishness and wield no powers of corruption. We ought to have our own class-consciousness."[25]

Wolin responds: "James says that intellectuals need their 'own class consciousness,' but before that he says that there are no interests and selfishness. Would the formation of class consciousness not lead to the formation of corporate selfishness, and do teachers not have tremendous powers of corruption? A reader would want to know why James's sceptical powers suddenly are suspended."[26] By "class consciousness," James did not imply material interests or the formation of teacher unions but was using the political vernacular to state something like, We should recognize that we are intellectuals and be proud of that fact, despite the attacks of anti-intellectuals, because we have a public contribution to make. The present danger is that intellectuals are not reaching audiences outside the academy and are exclusively interested in concocting ideals rather than ensuring that those ideals are realized in the world. His overstatement that intellectuals have no "corporate selfishness" may have been a function of the rhetoric: calls for change often lack doubt.

Like Plato, James placed education at the center of his scheme for social transformation. In *The Republic* and according to James's plan, leaders would be qualified by their learning. Of course, the theories of the two men are quite different. According to an old-fashioned reading of *The Republic*, Plato imagined well-trained philosophers who would apprehend the truth in the forms and govern society according to what they see.[27] The conflicts and power struggles at the heart of politics would be eliminated because the correct path would be apprehended by the philosophers and their authority would be undisputed by the many. A significant component of his educational plan and proposed social arrangements is to prepare the people to accept them.

Unlike Plato, James was committed to citizen action and to voting, implying that he respected the average citizen's capacity for courage and commitment to the common good.[28] For James, "geniuses" are characterized, not by what they know, but by the quality of their minds and temperament. By teaching the teachers of the many, the geniuses will transmit their qualities to the people and thus prepare them for self-government, which means in large part that the people will become capable of recognizing "good men" to serve as political leaders. For both James and Plato, philosophers embody the brain and reason of the country while the many tend to be guided by instinct or desire.[29] James did not want to destroy the people's spirit, he wanted it ruled by reason. Both Plato and James criticized political and economic institutions that inflame covetousness and undermine reason. The college-educated, in James's approach, like Plato's philosopher-kings, help reason ascend over passion, and thereby produce sagacious public decisions.

Not unlike traditional images of the political theorist, James's "geniuses" would lead the culture forward by interpreting both history and the present in new ways, providing visions of new and more generous institutions and policies, and disseminating a magnanimous temperament that would dampen the popular instinct for war.[30] Imagination, critical perspective, and the ability to reason would be disseminated by genius-professors to their graduate students in universities who would become college professors; college professors would prepare high school and elementary school teachers. The transformation of the country begins with "the reflective members of the State, and spreads slowly outward and downward."[31] Students trained in graduate schools would be the most contemplative, creative, and intelligent citizens. The healthy effects of education would be widely distributed among the population by "inoculating as many young Americans as possible with a general culture of the college grade," and professors would extend their benign influence on the nation via their students.[32]

> Such men are the backbone of the country. And no one can question the advantage to the country of having the largest possible number of them go to college, broaden their intellectual outlook, gain the sense of kinship with intellectual things, become once for all members of the free-masonry of the Educated, and continue to be voters for ideal interests during the remainder of their life.[33]

James did not always clearly distinguish between geniuses and teachers since he anticipated that the former would pass their "spark" on to the latter and through them to their students. It may be elitist to distinguish geniuses from ordinary people but egalitarian to hold that the many are capable of being influenced by the geniuses; and it is democratic to call for the spread of college education to everyone with the capacity for study.

American college students should come "from all degrees and ranks of society," not just the wealthy. James compared U.S. colleges favorably with Oxford and Cambridge because the latter "are, on the whole, aristocratic and not democratic schools."[34] Of course, not everyone has the intellect, wish, or funds to attend university, but the masses of people would still be affected by geniuses when they were taught in high school and grammar school by the college students who had had direct encounters with the geniuses or students of geniuses.[35] Because of their crucial function of disseminating the democratic temperament, "the teachers of this country, one may say, have its future in their hands."[36]

How would these teachers be developed? In essence, college students would learn by coming into contact with exceptional books and teachers.[37]

> It is the quality of its men that makes the quality of a university. You may have your buildings, you may create your committees and boards and regulations, you may pile up your machinery of discipline and perfect your methods of instruction, you may spend money till no one can approach you, yet you will add nothing but one more trivial specimen to the common herd of American colleges, unless you send into all this organization some breath of life, by inoculating it with a few men at least who are real geniuses.[38]

To say that there should be a few geniuses indicates that the task of education will be carried on by many who are not geniuses but who are educated. Nevertheless, the process of transmitting the spirit of geniuses to ordinary people is made complicated precisely because of the distinction James made between them. Will the ordinary folks listen to and be capable of receiving the teaching of the geniuses? In a paper supporting a proposal at Harvard to reduce the number of years at college from four to three, James acknowledged the gulf between the people who are committed to ideas and practical people, who will be touched by the scholarly temperament but will not become scholars. James did not believe that the aim of education is to make all students "intellectuals," and since contemplation is not the natural temper of most students, it would be fruitless to try to transform them. Such an exercise frustrates both the student and the professor. "Listlessness, apathy, dawdling, sauntering, the smoking of cigarettes and living on small sarcasms . . . are the direct fruit of keeping these men too long from contact with that world of affairs to which they rightfully belong."[39]

What could induce practical people to take advice, within the university and without, from scholars? What would give the geniuses authority? James thought academic style must change to attract popular interest. The curriculum should not be arcane but speak to subjects in a lively way. Whereas many people see colleges as exhibiting "a kind of sterilized conceit and incapacity for being pleased," colleges need to become robust and hearty because "if a college, through the inferior human influences that have grown regnant there, fails to catch the robuster tone, its failure is colossal, for its social function stops: democracy gives it a wide berth, turns toward it a deaf ear."[40]

In college, the curriculum should help to form democratic students, ironically by giving them an appreciation of excellence. James lived in a time when the terms "masterpieces," "excellence," "superiority," and "great deeds" were not impugned as being inherently antidemocratic or culturally biased. He stressed the truths and standards of great books, saying that at college, students should learn respect for the first-rate and disdain for the trashy and impermanent (108). The aim of colleges is to promote "the higher culture."[41] College, James said, teaches what "superiority" is. "Universities are already a sort of agency providentially provided for the detection and encouragement of mental superiority."[42]

Although James did not believe in a canon and argued for broadening the college curriculum to include modern works, he maintained that students should learn the nature of excellence by reading "masterpieces" of thought and studying great historic deeds. Masterpieces stimulate the mind while promoting standards of excellence and visions of alternative societies.[43] In language highly unfashionable today, and not particularly pluralist, James postulated that great books contain standards for action. "The ceaseless whisper of the more permanent ideals, the steady tug of truth and justice, give them but time, *must* warp the world in their direction" (110). By studying history, which describes the activities that "have stood the test of time; we acquire standards of the excellent and durable" (108). Wolin remarks: "This is a very old fashioned notion that goes back to the eighteenth century and earlier. It was always summarized by the popularity of Plutarch in the education of gentlemen because Plutarch has a series of great lives and great men who were supposed to serve as models."[44] James's traditional conception of education exposes his faith in truth and the progressive direction of history.

James tempered the elitism of his paean to excellence in two ways. First, he called for sympathy with people's mistakes and the pathos of lost causes.[45] Then he said that great books were not the only source of an education in excellence; people who did not attend college should receive a trade education, which also confers upon its students the means to recognize quality in fine workmanship. That knowledge would impart the ability to recognize and respect excellence in politicians.

It is not immediately apparent how teachers might follow James's advice today in shaping the curriculum. And even after his caveat to remember and empathize with the losers, one wonders if a steady diet of the excellent and extraordinary in college prepares students to appreciate their fellow citizens. As I showed earlier, James was torn on this issue, alternately praising the heroic pursuit of excellence and criticizing the American obsession with "the bitch-goddess Success."[46] This is not to say that James equated excellence and success; success can be attained by standards lower than excellence.

Having explicated James's theory of geniuses and the process of creating them, I would suggest that his theory is not as elitist as it first appears, and I will assess it by employing three criteria: its stated purposes, the method of selecting the geniuses, and the relationship of the many with the few. I argue that the elitist language James employed belies an egalitarian intention. He showed that a certain kind of elitism, the search for excellence in intellectual and political leadership and its dissemination among the many, is compatible with democracy.

James's democratic intention can better be discerned by looking at the political and historical contexts of his theory. The "anti-Dreyfus craze" fomented popular cries against *les intellectuals*; aristocrats indicted American populist impulses for undermining knowledgable guidance in public affairs; and the masses did appear to possess a hearty appetite whetted by demagogues for imperialist wars. Against these challenges, James affirmed that intellectuals serve the crucial function of moral and political leadership in a democratic society.[47] James has already been depicted as being unafraid of popular action, even militant conflict, but he did fear the populist impulse behind imperialism, lynching, and corruption in urban machines and national government. Instead of being restrained by public leaders, the human instinct for aggression was being incited by the tabloid press, Theodore Roosevelt, and other demagogues. The same dynamic occurs today when some politicians and public intellectuals play on widespread fears of crime, unemployment, poverty, and the temptation for children to use drugs or engage in promiscuity (and thus risk attendant diseases or unwanted pregnancy). Such leaders respond to these fears with calls for harsh punishment of criminals, a buildup of the military, invective toward real and imagined domestic and foreign enemies, and an end to affirmative action, welfare, and government support for education, the arts, and the humanities.

In the nineteenth century, James's friend Henry Adams expressed his belief that the Constitution of 1789 was outmoded, in part because it left power in the hands of the masses who were unqualified to wield it and because those who possessed sensitivity, perceptiveness, and restraint were excluded from positions of authority.[48] Such criticisms were at the heart of the Progressive call for civil service reform and the replacement of machine politics with managers. James conceded the force of these arguments, agreeing that democracy "may undergo self-poisoning," but he did not support the elimination of popular rule—on the contrary, he invoked faith in democracy, calling it "a kind of religion, and we are bound not to admit its failure." Democracy requires civic education so that citizens will act wisely and, above all, choose good leaders.[49] This is the first political purpose of education in excellence: to help citizens recognize and vote for representatives who embody the democratic temperament, i.e., who are committed to an active citizenry and mutual respect at home and abroad.[50]

Earlier in this chapter I showed that James's pedagogy was appropriate for direct democracy, and then I contrasted his pedagogical theory with a seemingly elitist formulation of the intellectual's function in society. I have tried to suggest that despite James's overly sharp division between intellectuals and other citizens, ultimately the purpose of intellectual leadership is to augment, not replace, democracy.

# IV

I began this chapter with a discussion of the need for a pedagogy that is appropriate to democracy. Teaching that relies upon the coercion of grades to elicit responses from students will only reinforce the passivity that teachers say they detest. Professors should use their authority to undermine student submissiveness, to wake them up. Certain teaching strategies, or forms of discipline, such as requiring students to speak in class, can be employed to motivate students to become active learners. As Rousseau might have said, professors need to force students to be free.

James provided a cautionary objection to my argument that coercion can be used democratically. He saw a danger in relying on it too much as a mode of teaching and, instead, urged professors to make their subjects engrossing to the students. "The genius of the interesting teacher consists in sympathetic divination of the sort of material with which the pupil's mind is likely to be already spontaneously engaged, and in the ingenuity which discovers paths of connection from that material to the matters to be newly learned. The principle is easy to grasp, but the accomplishment is difficult in the extreme."[51] Reliance on coercion to gain the students' attention "is a wasteful method, bringing bad temper and nervous wear and tear as well as imperfect results. The teacher who can get along by keeping spontaneous interest excited must be regarded as the teacher with the greatest skill."[52]

> Do not, then, for the mere sake of discipline, command attention from your pupils in thundering tones; do not too often beg it from them as a favor, nor claim it as a right, nor try habitually to excite it by preaching the importance of the subject. Sometimes, indeed, you must do these things; but the more you have to do them, the less skilful teacher you will show yourself to be.[53]

In place of stimulating student interest, teachers threaten students with low grades, including points off for absences, late submission of papers and tests, lack of participation in discussion, spelling and grammar errors, and failure to do assigned reading.

Forsaking coercion is, however, problematic. Students of teachers who have forsaken compulsion often use their freedom to avoid learning. How have things come to this point? Students who become accustomed to strict discipline in the early grades do not always adapt well to freedom later. They do not know how to work for something other than the grade, and they become extremely nervous when they are unsure what the teacher wants of them and when they are asked to develop their own ideas about a subject rather than presenting those of the author or professor.

A highly disciplinary model of pedagogy serves the needs of our economic and political system. Guided by their parents, many students use their college years to prepare for careers rather than pursuing intellectual interests. Colleges and universities, eager for the tuition dollars of a shrinking pool of students, most of whom are anxious about their future, try to accommodate demands for vocational courses such as advertising in the Art Department, journalism in English, law in Political Science, and accounting and business in Economics. Students then complain of boredom in classes they did not really care about in the first place, and which do not speak to their curiosity or larger questions of meaning; students are at other times impatient with courses that lack immediate relevance to their job aims or to negotiating "the real world." The conception has become rare in the enterprise of higher learning that students might not use their undergraduate years primarily to prepare for a place in the world, but develop a critical perspective on that world, and even attempt to shape it according to ideals acquired from their education. Unfortunately, the students do not complain enough about excessive discipline, which they assume to be part of the price that must be paid for success. Such students will probably not assume leadership roles in democratizing American politics and civil society.

In the spirit of James's teachings about education, I would like to put forward some suggestions for democratic change, even though I realize that the maxims and the proposals that follow will seem old hat to anyone interested in educational reform since the beginning of the century. I was lucky to attend first a progressive high school that employed Deweyan teaching methods and later the University of California, Santa Cruz, which had no grades, no textbooks, rare examinations, few firm deadlines for papers, and no attendance requirements. The university teachers assumed that the students had come to learn, and in most cases that assumption was correct. I heard many splendid lectures, but questions and challenges to the teachers' positions were welcomed.

I have now taught for a number of years in more traditional institutions and have found the students, overall, more inert and the professors more disciplinary and less experimental. Innovation now seems to mean "group projects." Textbooks and examinations are the norm. Students groan that they are required to sit through endless lectures without being given the opportunity to react, and they should object more than they do about being able to graduate from college without having to encounter great works of philosophy, history, literature, religion, and psychology. The idea of student participation in governing specific departments and the university itself has largely been dropped. Student evaluations, distributed and completed by rote, are what remains of the call for "student power" that became popular in the sixties.

Given the present situation, it seems useful to articulate again the principles of democratic teaching. They include the disruption of inherited ideas by questioning, indirection, and the presentation of alternative worldviews; challenging students to become independent thinkers and political actors by having them read significant books that are meaningful to the professor and potentially so to the students; sharing as much power as possible with the students; and finally, having sympathy with and affection for the students.

Translating these Jamesian principles into concrete reforms, here are some suggestions. First, James called for students to experience "great" authors and books. Even recognizing that the term "great" is highly contested and has been invoked in heated debates over expanding the canon, perhaps both traditionalists and innovators can agree that the resurgence of textbooks which, with few exceptions, are not brilliantly written should be questioned. Their very emphasis on clarity and neutrality induces mental laziness in the process of acquiring knowledge. Students should, for the most part, be exposed to powerful minds.

Second, reliance on examinations should also be reconsidered. Some exams rigorously challenge students and require them to pull together the various readings and ideas presented in the course, but too often testing demands only a restatement of the professor's ideas and the information in the text without eliciting a reaction from the student. Generally, it is better to allow students the time to write essays that analyze the text and respond to it. This recommendation is an amendment of James, who apparently took exams for granted.

Third, professors should require students to take an independent stand in writing papers and in commenting in class, or at least to state their difficulties in arriving at their own position. Students should not be rewarded for simply repeating the ideas of the professor or the text. This idea is in the spirit of James, who told students always to react to what they read and hear: "No reception without reaction, no impression without correlative expression—this is the great maxim which the teacher ought never to forget."[54]

Fourth, while making students aware of the classic works of Western civilization, the teacher must show the students how their concerns are addressed by authors of various countries, languages, periods, races, and genders, including their own. White male students can learn from nonwhite authors and from women writers just as women and people of color have always learned from white male writers. A multicultural education is particularly necessary in order to engender mutual respect in the diverse society of the United States. This point is a minor amendment of James, who believed in teaching powerful books in addition to the classics, and points in the direction of Dewey's multicultural classroom.

Fifth, outside the classroom, students should regularly participate in department meetings and serve on search committees. By participating more in the running of the university, students will better understand it, and upon graduation, become more articulate supporters of higher education. The more responsibility the students are given on campus, and the less they think of themselves as a subjugated group, the more lively they will be in the classroom. James explicitly called for students to take greater responsibility for student life on campus, so this proposal only expands his.

Sixth, academic departments and the administration should set an example for the students by being models of democratic decision making. Decisions should be made openly and with the involvement of the entire department, including the students. Democracy in the United States cannot be built from the top down, and we should start where we live and work. This suggestion supplements James's thinking.

These steps, among others, might help release the intellectual energy of the students, and invigorated students will be more likely to comprehend the world outside the college and to react to it in a humane and generous manner. Jamesian pedagogy would create citizens who are not content with merely voting for qualified representatives. Such students would not accept the lack of democracy in the United States and would critically analyze and challenge the hierarchical organization of politics, corporations, schools, and other institutions. Given the powerful economic and political forces that shape education, I, following James, may overemphasize the ability of professors to change the character of the citizenry and create democratic forms of politics and work in America. Yet it may be as Henry Adams counseled that "a teacher affects eternity; he can never tell where his influence stops."[55] On bad days, it is hard to tell where a teacher's influence begins. But why not try?

# Conclusion

## I

Various political regimes reflect and shape different temperaments among the citizenry. In a totalitarian society, for example, the citizens are generally isolated and fearful.[1] *The Oxford English Dictionary* defines "temperament" as a "constitution or habit of mind,"[2] and related words are character, disposition, and personality. We usually apply these words to individuals, but they can also pertain to a particular people, as when we say that southerners tend to be warm while New Englanders are more reserved.

James was preoccupied with two essential elements of a democratic temperament that he believed were appropriate for citizens of the United States: the inclination to action in the service of an ideal and mutual respect for all citizens and people in foreign countries, including those with different aims. He was by no means the first to talk about the values of democracy and mutual respect, but he articulated them well. He revealed a great deal of what is best in the American democratic tradition or character, much of which may be in danger of vanishing.

Citizens in a democracy cannot always rely on representatives, bureaucratic officials, or lawyers to act for them. Citizens need to say: "Don't do that for me; let me try. I want to have a hand in running it so let me learn how it's done." Tocqueville captured this aspect of the democratic temperament in *Democracy in America*:

> The inhabitant of the United States learns from birth that he must rely on himself to combat the ills and trials of life; he is restless and defiant in his outlook toward the authority of society and appeals to its power only when he cannot do without it. The beginnings of this attitude first appear at school, where the children, even in their games, submit to rules settled by themselves and punish offenses which they

112

have defined themselves. The same attitude turns up again in all the affairs of social life. If some obstacle blocks the public road halting the circulation of traffic, the neighbors at once form a deliberative body; this improvised assembly produces an executive authority which remedies the trouble before anyone has thought of the possibility of some previously constituted authority beyond that of those concerned. . . . [I]f an American should be reduced to occupying himself with his own affairs, at that moment half his existence would be snatched from him; he would feel it as a vast void in his life and would become incredibly unhappy.[3]

The second element of the democratic temperament is respect for other political actors, based in part on modesty about one's cause. I will now put James's position, to which I subscribe, into my own words. We act as if our causes were absolutely true, but James wanted us to temper that belief, to realize that we cannot locate an objective foundation for it. Discovering that we cannot find such foundations should lead us to two somewhat contradictory conclusions. First, we should not be paralyzed but instead comprehend that we can choose our campaigns without guarantees of their ultimate goodness or success. We cannot know for a long time, perhaps not in this life, whether or not we chose rightly. Second, because we do not possess certain knowledge that our cause is just, and we could be wrong, we should be more generous to our opponents. In this spirit, we might say: "This is how I see it, but I could be mistaken. It's only my best guess. The changes we want might make things worse—freedom of speech might permit fascism to flourish, the doctrine of localism could lead to ethnic fighting, school busing may provoke more segregation—but we hope that they will not, and we must run the risk. Try to see it my way, but if you don't, we will remain friends. Let's keep thinking and talking about the issue."

Tentativeness, acknowledgment of risk, self-doubt, and magnanimity toward opponents may sound idealistic and quite alien to the actual texture of political life. Political actors tend not to be wracked by doubt. And yet, democratic disputes are a part of ordinary politics and of everyday life, and politicians have to respond civilly to critics and the opposition. Teachers hear views, often from their favorite students, that give them pain. The professor might believe in community, but the student champions individualism. The teacher is a feminist, but the student clings to traditional gender roles. Even friends cannot agree on everything: one is a socialist, the other a capitalist; one eats no animals, another no animal products, and a third eats meat regularly. Somehow these friends dine together without rancor or completely burying the issues. Disagreements can become terrible—as when friends and families divided over the Vietnam War—but within families, in the classroom, among friends, and in the body politic, conflicts need to be tempered to prevent violence and dissolution of relationships. Conflicts can be restrained with a combination of humor, courtesy, respect, self-questioning, a thick skin, and recalling common bonds and areas of agreement. Such a democratic attitude is necessary, yet fragile, both for politics and society.

To say that there is a democratic temperament appropriate for all citizens will strike some readers as dangerous, particularly because James used gender-biased language to describe that temperament. He labeled the ideal citizen "manly" and the resigned person "feminine." In Chapter 2 I argued that despite his language, James believed both men and women could be energetic and active citizens. This ideal does not eliminate the problem that trying to mold citizens to a democratic temperament might be coercive. Some people do not want to participate, engage others in dialogue, or speak up when things are bothering them; they want to remain quiet, reflective, and uninterested in politics. True coercion, however, comes from the systems of command and obedience in the schools and in the workplace, and democratic authority conflicts with those hierarchical methods of shaping the character of the citizenry. I do not mean that shy people have no place in a democracy, but teachers and bosses should do everything they can to develop rather than quench the creative and active impulses of students and workers.[4]

James not only prescribed action and mutual respect but revealed their complexity and the difficulty of having them both at once. Preaching tolerance or mutual respect is easy enough, but those attributes are hard to achieve because most action is grounded in faith. James acknowledged that the usual cause of action is a person's fervently held beliefs. One person feels so strongly that Israel is endangering its future by giving back land won in war that he joins a demonstration to protest government policies. He believes that God has given the land to the Jewish people and that any government initiative to the contrary opposes God's will. This person potentially poses a problem for a democratic society. Democracies want their citizens to act on their beliefs but must perpetually draw the line between the fervent and the fanatical. Fanatics who believe that their aims are absolutely right, sanctioned by God, beyond doubt, and undisputable, are dangerous to democracy both because of the violence they may commit and because of the poisonous rhetoric they employ.

Although James argued that reason should be employed to temper differences—a key function of educators and political leaders—he was not sanguine about reason's capacity for mediation because most people hold ideas based on their emotions and personalities. And emotions tend to be both revealing of their objects ("I understand her more than you do because I care about her") and selfish ("I care about her, and everyone else can go hang"). Emotions tend to override reason and do not easily produce respect. The natural psychological inclination to disrespect means democracies must rely not only on citizen temperament but on the restraints of laws and institutions.

The mention of reason embodied by the college-educated and virtuous public leaders points to yet another seeming paradox in James and in democracy. Although people in a democracy should strive to respect everyone, achieving that goal requires leaders and teachers. Sometimes James writes as if only the few geniuses and great individuals matter in a society; at other times, he seems to value, even romanticize, the contribution of ordinary people. Clearly, James's nonelitist interpretation of authority is more useful for democracy. Democratic leaders and teachers moderate popular passions and encourage the people to elect virtuous leaders, but they also stimulate action and let the citizenry know that the nonheroic activities of attending to politics, studying the issues, and voting for honorable politicians are essential to preserving the body politic. Such a vigorous citizenry might design new ways to institutionalize participation and redistribute power from the center to the community.

During the last several years, there has been something of a pragmatist renaissance. Many books are being written and symposia being held on pragmatism, Dewey, Charles Peirce, and even James.[5] Richard Rorty, a prominent philosopher at the University of Virginia, and Cornel West of Harvard, perhaps the foremost African-American intellectual in the United States today, are at the center of the revival.

John Dewey (1859–1952) tends to get more attention from the neo-pragmatists than James does from people interested in politics, although Dewey himself acknowledged James's influence on his philosophical, political, and educational ideals. Dewey, a less-inspired writer, was more explicitly concerned with politics than James and put greater stress on the importance of community. Both men believed in the values of action and mutual respect. Like James, Dewey saw the school as a central institution for disseminating the democratic temperament and developed the conception of the school as a site where diverse groups of citizens could foster mutual respect by getting to know each other's cultures.[6] Dewey was far more optimistic than James about the capacity of scientific methods to guide government and technology in a healthy direction.[7]

Rorty uses pragmatism to justify liberalism in the United States. Toleration, overcoming cruelty, and solidarity with others would flow from the discovery of similarity between others and ourselves, and from the need to relieve pain.

> I want to distinguish solidarity as the identification with "humanity as such" and as the self-doubt which has gradually, over the last few centuries, been inculcated into inhabitants of the democratic states—doubt about their own sensitivity to the pain and humiliation of others, doubt that present institutional arrangements are adequate to deal with this pain and humiliation, curiosity about possible alternatives.[8]

Rorty undermines his call for doubt and solidarity by his peculiar use of a second theme from William James: the will to believe. Rorty infers from that will that Americans or people in any liberal democracy can champion their own political systems as the best even if they cannot prove its superiority. In this reworking of a Jamesian theme, there is a strain of cultural and political self-satisfaction that is rarely found in James. Rorty stakes out a position summarized as "postmodernist bourgeois liberalism," which he defines as the "attempt to defend the institutions and practices of the rich North Atlantic democracies without using [traditional Kantian] buttresses." Rorty exults, "Lately our species has been making up a particularly good nature for itself—that produced by the institutions of the liberal West." He identifies in human beings a "most advanced, sophisticated subspecies—the well-read, tolerant, conversable inhabitant of a free society."[9] If James praised the college-educated in similar language, he also criticized their tendencies toward blindness and a false sense of superiority. Rorty urges both reform and pride in the existing order but gives the impression that his heart is really with the status quo. In placing himself in the tradition of James and Dewey, Rorty understates the critical stances of both toward American political culture.

Cornel West preserves James's critical spirit, finding in pragmatism elements of a political and moral vision.[10] He characterizes pragmatism as an action-centered theory that respects the experiences of ordinary people and finds in it justification for democracy, individual freedom, worker self-management, and cultural heterogeneity. By contrast, bureaucracy, objectification, and commodification turn people into passive spectators. West sees in pragmatism a melding of Jefferson, Emerson, and Lincoln. Interpreting Jefferson and Emerson differently than I do, West finds in Jefferson individuality and community, in Emerson appreciation for the heroic action of ordinary people, and in Lincoln a deep sense of evil encountered in the fight for justice. West declares, "Unique selves acting in and through participatory communities give ethical significance to an open risk-ridden future," and he endorses the pragmatic idea that people determine the future through their own actions, not by triggering an inevitable historical process.[11]

As a theorist, West models himself after W. E. B. Du Bois, James's student. Pragmatism offers West an alternative to the dogmatic versions of Marxism, liberalism, and black nationalism, and he alternately labels the type of political theory and theorist he favors as "prophetic criticism," being a "critical organic catalyst," and "genealogical materialist analysis." Prophetic criticism exposes illegitimate authority, revealing how meaning is produced and mobilized to maintain domination. It perceives the dignity in ordinary lives while encouraging social experiments based on improvisation. The critical organic catalyst studies and takes the best ideas from the mainstream books; the theorist should tie the intellectual life with the best political forces in the community. West adopts prophetic pragmatism because it helps prophecy avoid the danger of dogmatism. Prophecy becomes self-critical, but retains moral outrage. He also maintains the prophetic element in his theory, drawn from Judaism and Christianity, because without it there would be a loss of "higher moral and political ground" for theorizing. "Genealogical materialist analysis" requires intellectuals, in addition to studying various texts, to turn their eyes to actual conditions in the world and the concrete history of those conditions. West's description of the theorist's vocation possesses a Jamesian spirit of moral seriousness.[12]

West disapproves of certain strains in pragmatism and distinguishes two political directions in it: the first linked with traditional liberalism and social engineering; the second, with political critique, social reform, and individual liberty. He claims that the neopragmatism associated with Rorty, like the old pragmatism, ignores power and understates the importance of inequality.[13]

I hesitate to find fault with Cornel West because I so greatly admire his generous vision, public activities, and conception of the theorist's vocation. He has attempted to act as a bridge between left-wing academics and the black community by trying to explain the preoccupations and vocabulary of each to the other. I do, however, have some concerns about West's work. He does not analyze in detail the texts he treats; he urges us to focus theoretical attention on power, but does not himself analyze it much; he lacks humor and irony; he does not acknowledge tensions and dilemmas in his own ideals or the sacrifices and risks implied in his political vision. He desires community and individualism and respects Farrakhan and the Jews, the working class, and new age morality. A few lines from James may be appropriate here: "Most of us have a hankering for the good things on both sides of the line [distinguishing contrary philosophical positions] . . . [But we] cannot preserve a good intellectual conscience so long as we keep mixing incompatibles from opposite sides of the line."[14] That said, I think West's description of pragmatism is essentially accurate, although he may understate James's potential contribution to the politics he endorses.

I have not tried to claim that James was a political theorist rather than a philosopher. Instead, I have argued that political concerns were central to his intellectual work and that studying James while remaining aware of those concerns is useful for political theorists and anyone interested in the future of democracy. James should be read for the elegance of his prose, his genius and generous spirit, and his insights into the possibilities and paradoxes of American democratic political consciousness.

He did not provide the analysis of power and institutions required by a complete political theory, but theory does not offer one-stop shopping, and other theorists such as Marx, Weber, and Tocqueville may be more useful on those themes. But James did specify the obstacles to equality and participation in the United States: the creation of large institutions, a natural drive toward elitism that requires constant restraint, and the overvaluing of material success. He confessed and tried to root out his own feelings of superiority while developing a language of respect for ordinary people that is appropriate for true democracy, a language that is at once demanding and appreciative of the heroic nature of everyday efforts. Among James's great contributions to American political thought is his analysis of political psychology, particularly the necessity and difficulty of achieving what I have called the democratic temperament: a vigorous citizenry respectful of differences among themselves and with other nations.

# NOTES

## Introduction

1. According to Bruce Kuklick, "James and [Josiah] Royce were not social and political thinkers of any stature" (*The Rise of American Philosophy: Cambridge, Massachusetts, 1860–1930* [New Haven: Yale University Press, 1977], 306).

2. Richard Hofstadter's statement is typical: "Unlike Dewey . . . James was guilty of only the remotest interest in systematic or collective social reform. One expression of his fundamental individualism is the fact that . . . he had no sustained interest in social theory as such" (*Social Darwinism in American Thought* [Boston: Beacon, 1955], 134). See also Henry Steele Commager, *The American Mind* (New Haven: Yale University Press, 1950), 99. On Dewey's political thought, see Robert B. Westbrook, *John Dewey and American Democracy* (Ithaca: Cornell University Press, 1991), and Alan Ryan, *John Dewey and the High Tide of American Liberalism* (New York: W. W. Norton, 1995). Deborah J. Coon offers an interesting comparison of James and Dewey in "Courtship with Anarchy: The Socio-Political Foundations of William James's Pragmatism" (Ph.D. diss., Harvard University, 1988). She argues that James's ideas were less compatible with the Progressive movement than Dewey's because James believed that "liberty and equality would best be attained *without* institutional interference. In fact, for James, the Progressives' increasing standardization and rationalization of society was anathema to liberty" (5 n.8).

3. On James's public career, the development of his political ideas, and the relationship of his philosophy to his politics, see two studies by intellectual historians: George Cotkin, *William James, Public Philosopher* (Baltimore: Johns Hopkins University Press, 1990), and Coon, "Courtship with Anarchy."

4. On Godkin, see *The Letters of William James*, ed. Henry James, 2 vols. (Boston: Atlantic Monthly Press, 1920), 1:284.

5. Santayana, *Persons and Places: Fragments of Autobiography*, ed. William G. Holzberger and Herman J. Saatkamp, Jr. (Cambridge: MIT Press, 1987), 404. Santayana called the Declaration "a piece of literature, a salad of illusions." On Godkin's influence see Ralph Barton Perry, *The Thought and Character of William James*, 2 vols. (Boston: Little, Brown, 1935), 2:290, 294–95.

121

6. *The Will to Believe* (1897; reprint, New York: Dover, 1956). See Jeffrey Lustig, *Corporate Liberalism* (Berkeley: University of California Press, 1982), 150–94, and Cornel West, *The American Evasion of Philosophy: A Genealogy of Pragmatism* (Madison: University of Wisconsin Press, 1989), 54–68.

7. *Varieties of Religious Experience* (Cambridge: Harvard University Press, 1985), 287.

8. See W. E. B. Du Bois, *The Souls of Black Folk* (1903; reprint, New York: Penguin, 1989), and Booker T. Washington, *Up from Slavery* (New York: Carol Publishing, University Books, 1993).

9. See Henry Adams, *The Education of Henry Adams*, ed. Ernest Samuels (Boston: Houghton Mifflin, 1974). Cotkin, "From Hamlet to Habit," in *William James, Public Philosopher*, 40–72, discusses the importance of Hamlet in James's life and writings and as a widespread cultural metaphor for the inability to act.

10. In *Critical Elections and the Mainsprings of American Politics* (New York: Norton, 1970), Walter Dean Burnham describes 1898 and the defeat of the Populist party as the crucial election after which American citizens stopped voting in great numbers.

11. W. Y. P. Elliott, *The Pragmatic Revolt in Politics* (New York: Macmillan, 1928), 21.

12. *The Portable Machiavelli*, ed. and trans. Peter Bondanella and Mark Musa (New York: Penguin, 1979), chap. 25, p. 159. On fears of passivity in the late nineteenth century, see John Higham, *Strangers in the Land: Patterns of American Nativism, 1860–1925*, 2d ed. (New York: Atheneum, 1963), 135.

13. I discuss James's theory of democratic education in Chapter 5.

14. I take up James's theory of heroic leadership in Chapter 1.

15. Hannah Arendt, "On Humanity in Dark Times: Thoughts About Lessing," in Arendt, *Men in Dark Times* (New York: Harcourt, Brace, and World, 1968), 24–25.

16. See Randolph Bourne, "Transnational America," in Bourne, *The Radical Will*, ed. Olaf Hansen (New York: Urizen, 1977), 248–64, and Horace Kallen, "Democracy Versus the Melting Pot," *Nation* 100 (18, 25 February 1915): 190–94, 217–20; *Culture and Democracy in the United States* (1924; reprint, New York: Arno Press, 1970); *Cultural Pluralism and the American Idea* (Philadelphia: University of Pennsylvania Press, 1956).

17. The classic introduction to James's life and thought is Ralph Barton Perry, *The Thought and Character of William James*, 2 vols. (Boston: Little, Brown, 1935). Important biographies include Gay Wilson Allen, *William James* (New York: Viking, 1967), and R. W. B. Lewis, *The Jameses: A Family Narrative* (New York: Farrar, Straus, and Giroux, 1991).

18. Jean Strouse, *Alice James: A Biography* (Boston: Houghton Mifflin, 1980).

19. According to Coon, James maintained that "the intellectual, as the conscience and consciousness of society, could and should redirect the energies of society into constructive, ethically sound paths" ("Courtship with Anarchy," 138).

20. Lloyd Morris, *William James: Message of a Modern Mind* (New York: Charles Scribner's Sons, 1950), 69.

21. Gerald Myers, *William James: His Life and Thought* (New Haven: Yale University Press, 1986), 435–36. Perry characterized James as "a mugwump, an antiimperialist, a civil-service reformer, a Dreyfusite, an internationalist and a liberal" (*Thought and Character*, 2:290).

22. *William James, Essays, Comments, and Reviews* (Cambridge: Harvard University Press, 1987), 170–76, 192–93. "That [James] had the energy to be concerned with the position of blacks, women, immigrants, minorities in other countries, the care of the insane, vivisection, medical legislation, educational policy, the temperance movement, the imperialism and militarism of the Spanish-American War, the annexation of the Philippines, and the Monroe Doctrine is a remarkable feature of his life and thought" (Myers, *William James*, 429). In "William James—Warts and All" (*American Quarterly* 29 [Summer 1977]: 207–21), George R. Garrison and Edward H. Madden deprecate James's political activities, asserting that James was not "a significant reformer." His "individualism kept him from acting in concert with others through effective organizations to bring to bear cumulative pressure" (211). Conceding that he wrote strong letters against American imperialism in the Philippines and condemned lynching, they argue that James did not contribute to Reconstruction or to the campaign for civil service reform, nor did he offer significant aid to blacks, women, or the Irish. They charge that he was ignorant of political theory, naive about the causes of imperialism, and while not deeply prejudiced, indulged in racial stereotypes.

23. Perry, *Thought and Character*, 2:216. For James's relationship with Lutoslawski, see Coon, "Courtship with Anarchy," 103–14.

24. On the efforts of American intellectuals to expand their public role between 1890 and 1914, see Leon Fink, "The Fearsome Public: Democratic Disenchantment and the Advance of Learning" (Paper presented at the Culture and Democracy Conference, Reynolda House Museum of Modern Art, Winston-Salem, North Carolina, 22 April 1995).

25. For a comparison of James and Nietzsche, see Emile Durkheim, *Pragmatism and Sociology*, trans. J. C. Whitehouse, ed. John B. Allcock (New York: Cambridge University Press, 1983), 2–4.

26. *Varieties of Religious Experience*, 39.

27. Karl Jaspers, *Nietzsche*, trans. Charles F. Wallraff and Frederick J. Schmitz (Chicago: Henry Regnery Gateway, 1965), 9–10 (emphasis in original).

## 1. Models of Action

1. Sheldon S. Wolin, *Politics and Vision* (Boston: Little, Brown, 1960), 239–351.

2. Herbert Spencer, "Man Versus the State," in Spencer, *Political Writings,* ed. John Offer (New York: Cambridge University Press, 1994), 147–48.

3. Wilson Carey McWilliams, *The Idea of Fraternity in America* (Berkeley: University of California Press, 1973), 381; William Graham Sumner, *What Social Classes Owe to Each Other* (New York: Harper, 1883).

4. James's most powerful statements on these themes can be found in his essay "What Makes a Life Significant," in *Talks to Teachers on Psychology* (Cambridge: Harvard University Press, 1983), 150–67, and in *Pragmatism* (Cambridge: Harvard University Press, 1975), especially "Pragmatism and Religion," 131–44. Important commentaries on James's theory of action in the face of the despairing mood in the United States at the end of the nineteenth century include Don Browning, "William James's Philosophy of the Person: The Concept of the Strenuous Life," *Zygon* 10 (June 1975): 162–74; George Cotkin, *William James, Public Philosopher* (Baltimore: Johns Hopkins University Press, 1990), 95–122; and T. J. Jackson Lears, *No Place of Grace: Antimodernism and the Transformation of American Culture* (New York: Pantheon Books, 1981). Richard Flathman calls James "an enthusiastic voluntarist" (*Willful Liberalism: Voluntarism and Individuality in Political Theory and Practice* [Ithaca: Cornell University Press, 1992], 5). See also Ralph Barton Perry, *The Thought and Character of William James,* 2 vols. (Boston: Little, Brown, 1935), 2:478, 574.

5. See Sheldon S. Wolin, *Presence of the Past: Essays on the State and the Constitution* (Baltimore: Johns Hopkins University Press, 1989), and "Norm and Form: The Constitutionalizing of Democracy," in *Athenian Political Thought and the Reconstruction of American Democracy,* ed. J. Peter Euben, John R. Wallach, and Josiah Ober (Ithaca: Cornell University Press, 1994), 29–58.

6. "The Ghostly Body Politic: The Federalist Papers and Popular Sovereignty," in Joshua Miller, *Rise and Fall of Democracy in Early America* (University Park: Pennsylvania State University Press, 1991), 105–29.

7. *The Federalist,* ed. Jacob E. Cooke (Middletown, Conn.: Wesleyan University Press, 1961), 32, 61.

8. "The Importance of Individuals," in *The Will to Believe* (1897; reprint, New York: Dover, 1956), 260.

9. *Varieties of Religious Experience* (Cambridge: Harvard University Press, 1985), 72; see also *The Principles of Psychology,* 2 vols. (1890; reprint, Cambridge: Harvard University Press, 1981), 2:1138–44.

10. *Talks to Teachers,* 23–24.

11. "The Moral Equivalent of War," in *Essays in Religion and Morality* (Cambridge: Harvard University Press, 1982), 171.

12. Perry, *Thought and Character*, 2:290, 307–9; James, "The Social Value of the College-Bred," in *Essays, Comments, and Reviews* (Cambridge: Harvard University Press, 1987), 110–12; *The Letters of William James*, ed. Henry James, 2 vols. (Boston: Atlantic Monthly Press, 1920) 2:74.

13. Letter to Henry James, 10 April 1898, in *William and Henry, 1897–1910*, vol. 3 of *The Correspondence of William James*, ed. Ignas K. Skrupskelis and Elizabeth M. Berkeley (Charlottesville: University Press of Virginia, 1994), 26.

14. Letter to Theodore Flournoy, 17 June 1898, in Perry, *Thought and Character*, 308 (emphasis in original).

15. "The Moral Equivalent of War," 162–73.

16. The yearning for action and fear of passivity were not themes unique to James. Oliver Wendell Holmes and Theodore Roosevelt were but two other important members of the cult of action. James thought that his view and theirs were significantly different: Holmes's belief in action lacked ethical content and neglected to see the heroism in everyday life; Roosevelt dangerously linked action with war and imperialism. See Oliver Wendell Holmes, "Speech at a Dinner Given by the Bar Association of Boston," 7 March 1900, in *The Occasional Speeches of Justice Oliver Wendell Holmes*, ed. Mark DeWolfe Howe (Cambridge: Harvard University Press, 1962), 122–27, and Theodore Roosevelt, "The Strenuous Life," in *The Strenuous Life* (New York: Century, 1902), 1–21. James's critique of Holmes is in Perry, *Thought and Character*, 2:251. James criticized his former student in "An Answer to Roosevelt on the Venezuelan Crisis (1896)" and "Governor Roosevelt's Oration (1899)," in *Essays, Comments, and Reviews*, 152–53, 162–66. I compare James with Roosevelt and Holmes again in Chapter 2.

17. James's theory of mutual respect, discussed in Chapter 4, described the appropriate limits on action.

18. Cf. Hannah Arendt's emphasis on action for its own sake, not the outcome (*The Human Condition* [Chicago: University of Chicago Press, 1958], 7–21, 175–247).

19. James to Theodore Flournoy, 7 December 1896, *The Letters of William James and Theodore Flournoy*, ed. Robert C. Le Clair (Madison: University of Wisconsin Press, 1966), 62.

20. 9 May 1886, *William and Henry, 1885–1896*, vol. 2 of *The Correspondence of William James*, ed. Ignas K. Skrupskelis and Elizabeth M. Berkeley (Charlottesville: University Press of Virginia, 1993), 40. "The National Labor Union (NLU) and the Knights of Labor . . . were broadly reformist, industrial unions that sought to unite all segments of the work force (agricultural and industrial, skilled and unskilled) and to supplant the wage system with worker-owned 'producer coop-

eratives.' . . . The Knights flourished briefly in the late 1870s and early 1880s and had 750,000 members at peak strength. . . . In 1886 at a labor rally in Chicago's Haymarket Square, a bomb killed and injured police; the Knights were unjustly associated with the incident in the public mind. The union lost members and perished in the depression of the 1890s. Its major competitor and successor was the American Federation of Labor" (Charles Sellers, Henry May, Neil R. McMillen, *A Synopsis of American History*, 6th ed. [Boston: Houghton Mifflin, 1985], 257–58).

21. 16 March 1909, *Letters of William James*, ed. Henry James, 1:321.

22. See Arendt, *The Human Condition*, and "What Is Freedom?" in Arendt, *Between Past and Future* (New York: Penguin, 1961), 143–71; George Kateb, "The Theory of Political Action," in *Hannah Arendt: Politics, Conscience, Evil* (Totowa, N.J.: Rowman and Allanheld, 1983), 1–51; Wendy Brown, *Manhood and Politics: A Feminist Reading in Political Theory* (Totowa, N.J.: Rowman and Littlefield, 1988), 23–29; and Hanna Fenichel Pitkin, "Justice: On Relating Public and Private," *Political Theory* 9 (August 1981): 327–52.

23. I am thinking of Aristotle's formulation that humans fulfill their telos in the political life of a community and am trying to avoid an association with the currently popular language of personal growth. The suggestion that public activity can be fulfilling does not mean that politics should be seen as part of the self-help movement.

24. Arendt is at her most democratic in *The Human Condition* and in *Crises of the Republic* (New York: Harcourt Brace Jovanovich, 1972). She is far less democratic when she supports the Federalists and criticizes the Antifederalists for being anti-institutionalists in *On Revolution* (New York: Viking, 1962). See Miller, *Rise and Fall*, 9–10, 61.

25. Perry, *Thought and Character*, 2:315–16.

26. "Robert Gould Shaw: Oration by Professor William James," in *Essays in Religion and Morality*, 73–74.

27. Quoted in Lloyd Morris, *William James: Message of a Modern Mind* (New York: Charles Scribner's Sons, 1950), 74.

28. "Politics as a Vocation," *From Max Weber*, trans. and ed. H. H. Gerth and C. Wright Mills (New York: Oxford University Press), 82, 95, 93–95, 77, 115.

29. Perry, *Thought and Character*, 2:574.

30. *Talks to Teachers*, 164.

31. In rereading Marx recently, I was struck by similarities between Marx and James on the theme of thought and action. Like James, Marx demanded action, asserting that merely changing consciousness was ineffectual. Also, Marx said in "Theses on Feuerbach" that truth was not to be discovered in the world but ac-

complished through practice. The possibility of meaningful work, for example, is not a philosophical question but a call for society to create it. James expressed this same sentiment repeatedly.

32. Browning, "William James's Philosophy of the Person," 163. Christopher Lasch said that the sick soul described by James in *Varieties of Religious Experience* becomes the "strenuous lover of life" (*The True and Only Heaven* [New York: Norton, 1991], 292).

33. Intellectual historian Bruce Kuklick disagrees, denigrating James, Josiah Royce, and Charles S. Peirce as being apolitical, although he claims that "both Royce and James popularized their moral and religious ideas." Kuklick writes: "George Santayana put it well, if acerbically, when he said of the Harvard philosophers that they had an acute sense of social responsibility 'because they were conscientiously teaching and guiding the community, as if they had been clergymen without a church . . . at once genuine philosophers and popular professors.' " Yet, Kuklick concludes: "Whatever their concern for ethics and religion, James and Royce gave little time to social and political philosophizing. Their output in these areas was slight, their analyses lacked intellectual substance, and their applications were conventional and often trivial" (Bruce Kuklick, *The Rise of American Philosophy: Cambridge, Massachusetts, 1860–1930* [New Haven: Yale University Press, 1977], 306–7). Obviously, I disagree with Kuklick's conclusion.

34. "Social Value of the College-Bred," 111. By "inferior human influences" James may have meant priggishness and fear.

35. Arendt, *The Human Condition*, 178–79. The similarity between James and Arendt on this point comes from Wolin's editorial comments.

36. On the public/private distinction, see Carole Pateman, *The Disorder of Women: Democracy, Feminism, and Political Theory* (Stanford: Stanford University Press, 1989), 118–40.

37. *Talks to Teachers*, 163.

38. "Action, therefore, could be defined as an internal effort which had little to do with physical activity. It was the kind of heroism that keeps sensitive and thoughtful men from suicide, not the kind that wins battles" (George Fredrickson, *The Inner Civil War: Northern Intellectuals and the Crisis of the Union* [New York: Harper and Row, 1965], 232).

39. *Talks to Teachers*, 163–64. See also Browning, "William James's Philosophy of the Person," 163–64.

40. He wrote, "The solid meaning of life is always the same eternal thing—the marriage, namely, of some unhabitual ideal, however special, with fidelity, courage, and endurance; with some man's or woman's pains" (*Talks to Teachers*, 166).

41. *Letters of William James*, ed. Henry James, 1:130–31 (emphasis in origi-

nal). In "The Moral Equivalent of War," James mentions "dish-washing, clothes-washing, and window-washing . . . road-building and tunnel-making" (*Essays in Religion and Morality,* 172).

42. "What Makes a Life Significant," 161, 161–62, 163.

43. *Will to Believe,* 218, 137–38, 145–46, 227; see also James, *The Principles of Psychology,* 2:1235, and Browning, "William James's Philosophy of the Person," 164.

44. See Sumner, *What Social Classes Owe to Each Other,* and Henry Adams, *The Education of Henry Adams,* ed. Ernest Samuels (1918; reprint, Boston: Houghton Mifflin, 1974), 224–36 and passim. Grant Allen (1848–1899) was a prolific novelist and writer about Darwin and evolution (*Who Was Who in America,* vol. 1, *1897–1942* [Chicago: A. N. Marquis Company, 1942]). Allen visited James in New Hampshire in 1886 (Perry, *Thought and Character,* 1:604). For Grant Allen's direct response to James's criticisms of him, see "The Genesis of Genius," *Atlantic Monthly* 47 (March 1881): 371–81. Richard Hofstadter's *Social Darwinism in American Thought* (Boston: Beacon, 1955) is the classic work on its subject.

45. Political theorist John H. Schaar's work has been in large part devoted to the analysis of the causes for withdrawal from politics and to exhorting his fellow citizens to join public life. See especially his essay "Power and Purity" in Schaar, *Legitimacy in the Modern State* (New Brunswick, N.J.: Transaction Books, 1981), 313–30.

46. Hofstadter, *Social Darwinism,* 133. See *Will to Believe,* 236. Hofstadter added, "The pragmatists' most vital contribution to the general background of social thought was to encourage a belief in the effectiveness of ideas and the possibility of novelties—a position necessary to any philosophically consistent theory of social reform" (125). Philosopher Henry D. Aiken said that according to James, "The world, and man as a central being in the world, is malleable, subject to mutations brought about by the determined decisions and actions of ordinary human beings" ("William James as Moral and Social Philosopher," *Philosophic Exchange* 3 [Summer 1980]: 58).

47. "Rationality, Activity, and Faith," *Princeton Review* 2 (July 1882): 77; see also *Will to Believe,* 150, 235, and Hofstadter, *Social Darwinism,* 125, 132. "Great Men" and "The Dilemma of Determinism" are in *Will to Believe,* 145–83, 216–54.

48. *Will to Believe,* 246, 251.

49. Ibid., 218, 150. Note that James's list of historical agents includes both leaders and ordinary citizens.

50. *Pragmatism,* 137–38 (emphasis in original).

51. Ibid., 138, 139.

52. William James, *The Principles of Psychology*, 2:1235; *Will to Believe*, 226, 248, 260. The account of Darwinism is drawn from Browning, "William James's Philosophy of the Person," 164–65. Cotkin distinguishes James from Nietzsche, saying that James believed most people could not be overmen and that God was needed for most people to act (*William James*, 102–3). But James sometimes seems to agree with Nietzsche that only the few count, and James's antifoundationalism comes close to atheism.

53. *Will to Believe*, 227.

54. *Talks to Teachers*, 152.

55. Ibid., 159.

56. *Will to Believe*, 247–48, 100.

57. Perry insightfully claims in *Thought and Character*: "The heat which he missed in Emerson, William James found in Carlyle. The essays published in 1898 under the title of *The Will to Believe* [which includes "Great Men and Their Environment"] were composed in part as early as 1879, and they prove how deeply in his youth their author had drunk of Carlyle" (1:145). In *American Monroe* (Berkeley: University of California Press, 1995), S. Paige Baty's discussion of Emerson on the great man and masses dialectic is highly reminiscent of James (88–89).

58. Coon, "Courtship with Anarchy: The Socio-Political Foundations of William James's Pragmatism" (Ph.D. diss., Harvard University, 1988), 67, 81–84, 114, 122–218; Cotkin, *William James*, 124; James, "Social Value of the College-Bred," 106–12.

59. "The Social Value of the College-Bred," 108–10. Note that James shifts his own identification between being one of the elite ("we alumni") and one of the many ("the rest of us"). For the type of view James is repudiating, see Adams, *Education of Henry Adams*, 248–49, 280–81. One can read Adams's suggestion that the Constitution is outmoded as a rejection of democracy on the grounds that a corrupt American public cannot choose competent and moral leaders.

60. "Robert Gould Shaw," 66–67. See also *Talks to Teachers*, 154–56.

61. "Robert Gould Shaw," 66, 72, 73.

62. This self-hatred may be largely confined to people raised in activist eras such as the Civil War, the Roosevelt era, or the sixties, but I have also detected it in some of my students.

63. See James in Perry, *Thought and Character*, 2:250–51.

64. *Will to Believe*, 242–43.

65. "Developing Community Leadership: Ella Baker," in *Black Women in White America*, ed. Gerda Lerner (New York: Vintage, 1973), 348. Baker cautioned against excessive reliance on leadership saying, "I have always felt it was a handicap for oppressed peoples to depend so largely upon a leader, because unfor-

tunately in our culture, the charismatic leader usually becomes a leader because he has found a spot in the public limelight" (351).

66. Ibid., 352.

67. Starhawk, *Truth or Dare: Encounters with Power, Authority, and Mystery* (New York: Harper San Francisco, 1990), 269. On discussions of leadership in new feminist and antinuclear movements, see Barbara Epstein, *Political Protest and Cultural Revolution* (Berkeley: University of California Press, 1991).

68. *Will to Believe*, 260–61.

69. Cornel West also called for leadership: "There is no one who is willing to be prophetic in a bold and defiant manner with a deep, all-inclusive moral vision and a sophisticated analysis of the distribution of wealth and power and resources in our society" (Cornel West and Bell Hooks, *Breaking Bread* [Boston: South End Press, 1991], 48).

70. Clayborne Carson, *In Struggle: SNCC and the Black Awakening of the 1960s* (Cambridge: Harvard University Press, 1981), 139, 171.

71. Ibid., 303.

72. Political theorist W. Y. P. Elliott wrote that "only a romanticist can follow James as far as he leads in the direction of . . . irrationalism and pluralistic individualism" (*The Pragmatic Revolt in Politics* [New York: Macmillan, 1928], 46). Philosopher John J. McDermott said that "few thinkers have had James's confidence in the capacity of individuals to transform their world by tapping the energy of a voluntaristic ethic. . . . Nevertheless . . . the individual is a social category, contexted over and over again by the swirling factors of institutional and communal history" (*The Writings of William James*, ed. John J. McDermott [Chicago: University of Chicago Press, 1977], xi). See also ibid., xi–xiii.

73. Flathman, *Willful Liberalism*, 5; see also 69–70. In "William James as Moral and Social Philosopher," Aiken said that in contrast to Royce and Peirce, James was an individualist (55).

74. Comel West, *The American Evasion of Philosophy* (Madison: University of Wisconsin Press, 1989), 60. West says that James possessed "apolitical notions of how to change the world" (59).

75. Hofstadter, *Social Darwinism*, 134.

76. See Gerald E. Myers, *William James: His Life and Thought* (New Haven: Yale University Press, 1986), 439–42.

77. Santayana, *Persons and Places: Fragments of Autobiography*, ed. William G. Holzberger and Herman J. Saatkamp, Jr. (Cambridge: MIT Press, 1987), 403.

78. Gary Jacobsohn, *Pragmatism, Statesmanship, and the Supreme Court* (Ithaca: Cornell University Press, 1977), 45 n.15; Fredrickson, *Inner Civil War*, 237. One might think of the Populists and Edward Bellamy, as well as Progressives like Herbert Croly in *The Promise of American Life* (New York: Macmillan, 1909), who

criticized individualism. See McWilliams, *The Idea of Fraternity in America*, 469–506.

79. James to William Salter, 11 September 1899, *Letters of William James*, ed. Henry James, 2:100–101 (emphasis in original).

80. *Talks to Teachers*, 4.

81. Alexis de Tocqueville, *Democracy in America*, ed. J. P. Mayer, trans. George Lawrence (Garden City, N.Y.: Doubleday, 1969), 506.

82. "The Dilemma of Determinism," 174–75; *Pragmatism*, 139.

83. In *Essays in Religion and Morality*, 169.

84. James to Thomas Ward, January 1868, *Letters of William James*, ed. Henry James, 1:132 (emphasis in original). See also *Varieties of Religious Experience*, 299; *Will to Believe*, 232; "Robert Gould Shaw," 72; Browning, "William James's Philosophy of the Person," 170.

85. "Thomas Davidson: Individualist," in *Essays, Comments, and Reviews*, 86–97. Davidson (1840–1900) was a "philosopher and wandering scholar" who was born into a poor family in Scotland, studied classics in college, taught public school in St. Louis, and fell in with neo-Hegelians there who influenced him to reject positivism without embracing Hegel. He taught men and women from the Lower East Side in association with the People's Institute and the Educational Alliance of New York and went on to organize "a Bread-Winners' College" to bring the fruits of higher culture to wage earners (*Dictionary of American Biography*, vol. 5, ed. Allen Johnson and Dumas Malone [New York: Charles Scribners' Sons, 1946]). On the relationship of Davidson and James, see Perry, *Thought and Character*, 1:731–61, and Coon, "Courtship with Anarchy," 84–102.

86. Myers, *William James*, 430; Hofstadter, *Social Darwinism*, 135; McDermott, "Introduction," in *Writings of William James*, xxxi–ii. James may be close to George Kateb's notion of democratic individuality described in *The Inner Ocean* (Cornell University Press, 1992).

87. "Thomas Davidson: Individualist," 94.

88. In *Essays in Religion and Morality*, 170. In "What Makes a Life Significant," in *Talks to Teachers on Psychology*, James asserts, "the distribution of wealth has doubtless slowly got to change" (166). James's socialism was influenced by Fourier, through his father Henry James, Sr., and H. G. Wells (Perry, *Thought and Character*, 1:60, 2:289; Myers, *William James*, 439). In a passage interesting for what it says about James's way of thinking, James paraphrased Wells's defense of socialism in *New Worlds for Old:* "The commonest vice of the human mind is its disposition to see everything as yes or no, as black or white, its incapacity for discrimination of intermediate shades. So the critics agree to some hard and fast definition of socialism, and extract absurdities from it as a conjurer gets rabbits from a hat. Socialism abolishes property, abolishes the family, and the rest. The

method, Mr. Wells continues, is always the same: It is to assume that whatever the socialist postulates as desirable is wanted without limit of qualification . . . it is to imagine that whatever proposal is made by him is to be carried out by uncontrolled monomaniacs, and so to make a picture of the socialist dream which can be presented to the simple-minded person in doubt—'This is socialism'—or pluralism, as the case may be. 'Surely!—SURELY! you don't want *this*' " (William James, *A Pluralistic Universe* [Cambridge: Harvard University Press, 1977], 40). Cotkin rejects the notion that James was a socialist of any kind, labeling him an "existential anarchist" (*William James*, 172–75).

89. Sheldon Wolin comments: "Is his individualism so concerned with leaving a place for action as it is allowing variety to flourish even to the point of welcoming eccentricity? That's a different emphasis than other writers take with individualism. The starting point for James's individualism is his pluralism, not a kind of atomism. Pluralism suggests that while there are differences and variety, there are also webs of affiliation between the differences" (Wolin editorial comment).

90. Substantiation for these points can be found in Wolin, *Presence of the Past*, and Miller, *Rise and Fall of Democracy in Early America*.

## 2. James and Gender

1. *Varieties of Religious Experience* (Cambridge: Harvard University Press, 1985), 45.

2. "Moral Equivalent of War," in *Essays in Religion and Morality* (Cambridge: Harvard University Press, 1982), 170. See also letter to Henry James, 22 September 1893, in *William and Henry, 1885–1896*, vol. 2 of *The Correspondence of William James*, ed. Ignas K. Skrupskelis and Elizabeth M. Berkeley (Charlottesville: University Press of Virginia, 1993), 240.

3. "Moral Equivalent of War," 171 (emphasis in original). The term is misleading since in context James seems to refer to cleaning, building, and hiking. On the dangers of masculine domination of nature, see *Reweaving the World: The Emergence of Ecofeminism*, ed. Irene Diamond and Gloria Orenstein (San Francisco: Sierra Club Books/Random House, 1990); Wendy L. Brown, *Manhood and Politics* (Totowa, N.J.: Rowman and Littlefield, 1988), 199–200; and Jane Roland Martin, "Martial Virtues or Capital Vices? William James's Moral Equivalent of War Revisited," *Journal of Thought* 22 (Fall 1987): 32–44; here citing p. 34.

4. Martin, "Martial Virtues," 39.

5. For a range of feminist thinking today, see Linda J. Nicholson, ed., *Feminism/Postmodernism* (New York: Routledge, 1990), and Marianne Hirsch and Evelyn Fox Keller, eds., *Conflicts in Feminism* (New York: Routledge, 1990). In this

chapter I draw on Brown, *Manhood and Politics*; Christine Di Stefano, *Configurations of Masculinity: A Feminist Perspective on Modern Political Theory* (Ithaca: Cornell University Press, 1991); Nancy C. M. Hartsock, "Prologue to a Feminist Critique of War and Politics," in *Women's Views of the Political World of Men*, ed. Judith H. Stiehm (Dobbs Ferry, N.Y.: Transnational Publishers, 1984), 121–50; Martin, "Martial Virtues"; Hanna Fenichel Pitkin, "Justice: On Relating Public and Private," *Political Theory* 9 (August 1981): 327–52; and Ann Popkin, "The Personal Is Political: The Women's Liberation Movement," in *They Should Have Served That Cup of Coffee*, ed. Dick Cluster (Boston: South End Press, 1979), 181–224.

6. See, for example, the striking difference between Wendy Brown's *Manhood and Politics* and her recent *States of Injury: Power and Freedom in Late Modernity* (Princeton: Princeton University Press, 1995).

7. Brown, *Manhood and Politics*, 172.

8. Di Stefano, *Configurations of Masculinity*, 60. She writes that greatly emphasizing "self-creative abilities" is "misogynist because it perpetuates a fear of and consequent need to dominate naturalized, and hence dangerous women" (129). She criticizes male autonomy on 164, 168, 173.

9. Ibid., 22.

10. Brown, *Manhood and Politics*, 25–26. This critique of masculinity implicitly links feminism with pragmatism's traditional emphasis on concrete ends over debates about abstract ideals.

11. Ironically, one of the clearest expressions of this distinction can be found in Hannah Arendt, *The Human Condition* (Chicago: University of Chicago Press, 1958). See Pitkin, "Justice," and Brown, *Manhood and Politics*, for feminist critiques of Arendt's distinction. In Chapter 1, I showed that James did not sharply differentiate public from private life and is thus close to radical feminism on this point.

12. "Male gender identity, Nancy Chodorow has argued, is based on difference from the mother" (Michael Paul Rogin, "The Great Mother Domesticated: Sexual Difference and Indifference in D. W. Griffith's Intolerance," in *Discovering Difference*, ed. Christoph K. Lohmann [Bloomington: Indiana University Press, 1993], 180). See Chodorow, *Reproduction of Mothering* (Berkeley: University of California Press, 1978), 106.

13. Di Stefano, *Configurations of Masculinity*, xiv; see also 157.

14. Several of Sheldon Wolin's and Carey McWilliams's editorial comments on the draft manuscript of this book seem worth citing directly. In commenting upon this passage, McWilliams asks: "Is there no connection created when boys identify with their fathers? And what happens to girls brought up by two gay men? How do they create their identities?" (McWilliams editorial comment).

15. Pitkin, "Justice," 341; Hartsock, "Prologue," 149.

16. Brown, Manhood and Politics, 116–17.

17. Hartsock, "Prologue," 149; Martin, "Martial Virtues," 39; Pitkin in "Justice," writes, "The appeal to heroism and glory unconnected to any standard of right transcending the individual is bound to produce at best empty posturing, at worst, violence and war" (341). See George Cotkin, William James, Public Philosopher (Baltimore: Johns Hopkins University Press, 1990), 126, 146, 148, on James's effort to break the tie between manly virtues and war. See also Christopher Lasch, The True and Only Heaven (New York: Norton, 1991), 283.

18. Hartsock, "Prologue," 123, also 143, 146; Brown, Manhood and Politics, 79.

19. Martin, "Martial Virtues," 34.

20. Brown attempts to answer this question in Manhood and Politics, 189–211. Pitkin in "Justice" describes a highly attractive form of democratic politics devoid of heroic display, but she does not specifically call this a feminist vision (343–48).

21. On women's psychology, see Carol Gilligan, In a Different Voice: Psychological Theory and Women's Development (Cambridge: Harvard University Press, 1982). On women's experience, see Sandra Lee Bartky, Femininity and Domination (New York: Routledge, 1990). See also Joan C. Tronto, Moral Boundaries: A Political Argument for an Ethic of Care (New York: Routledge, 1993), and Sara Ruddick, Maternal Thinking: Toward a Politics of Peace (Boston: Beacon, 1989).

22. Di Stefano, Configurations of Masculinity, 172. For a recent rendering of the violence in cowboy life, see Cormac McCarthy, All the Pretty Horses (New York: Knopf, 1992).

23. Command and obedience are sometimes necessary but they need not be perpetual. After the crisis, there is room for more discussion. On feminist practice, see Barbara Epstein, Political Protest and Cultural Revolution (Berkeley: University of California Press, 1991); Starhawk, Truth or Dare: Encounters with Power, Authority, and Mystery (New York: Harper San Francisco, 1990); and Popkin, "The Personal Is the Political."

24. Sheldon S. Wolin editorial comments.

25. Michael C. Adams, The Great Adventure: Male Desire and the Coming of World War I (Bloomington: Indiana University Press, 1990), is a powerful and lucid description of how men understood gender roles in the late nineteenth century. I was surprised to see how much James's vocabulary both reflected and deviated from the Victorian discourse of masculinity.

26. Elizabeth Scarborough and Laurel Furumoto, Untold Lives: the First Generation of American Women Psychologists (New York: Columbia University Press, 1987), 27–30, 35–36.

27. *The Principles of Psychology*, 2 vols. (Cambridge: Harvard University Press, 1891), 2:1033, 939, 1054.

28. *Varieties of Religious Experience*, 73; *Principles of Psychology* 2:991, 1054.

29. Charlotte Brontë, *Jane Eyre* (New York: New American Library/Signet, [1847]), 112–13.

30. See Gerald E. Myers, *William James: His Life and Thought* (New Haven: Yale University Press, 1986), 428–29. Martin, "Martial Virtues," would reject this line of argument, believing that James's discussion of "manliness" applied specifically to men (36, 42).

31. James to Margaret James, 26 May 1900, *Letters of William James*, ed. Henry James, 2 vols. (Boston: Atlantic Monthly Press, 1920), 2:130; emphasis added.

32. "One could say that women have taken James's advice here, especially since World War II, and thus have incorporated James's ideal of manliness" (Wolin editorial comments).

33. Early feminists expanded the political significance of motherhood in order to have a public role denied to them by men. There has been significant debate about whether this move was liberating or confining (Linda Kerber, *Women of the Republic: Intellect and Ideology in Revolutionary America* [Chapel Hill: University of North Carolina Press, 1980]).

34. *Varieties of Religious Experience*, 212. Similarly, James wrote in his *Principles of Psychology:* "The passionate devotion of a mother—ill herself, perhaps—to a sick or dying child is perhaps the most simply beautiful moral spectacle that human life affords. Contemning every danger, triumphing over every difficulty, outlasting all fatigue, woman's love is here invincibly superior to anything that man can show" (2:1056). Although the sentimentalism and emphasis on maternity may be a bit nauseating, it is undeniable that James attributes to women the capacity for being heroic, ascetic.

35. Letter to family, Dresden, 24 July 1867, in Ralph Barton Perry, *The Thought and Character of William James*, 2 vols. (Boston: Little, Brown, 1935), 1:239–40; letter to Mrs. Alice James, 24 September 1882, in *Letters of William James*, 1:211. The two statements of praise for the German peasant women are fifteen years apart, written when James was twenty-five and forty.

36. This insight, along with several others in this chapter, comes from Elaine Thomas's comments on an early draft.

37. Today, rhetoric against dependency is invoked as a justification for cutting welfare and other forms of aid to the poor, but it would be incorrect to attribute that motive to James in an era before the welfare state was created.

38. Myers, *William James*, 429.

39. *Essays, Comments, and Reviews* (Cambridge: Harvard University Press, 1987), 246–56; the quotations that follow can be found on pp. 255, 250, 251 (emphasis in original), and 252.

40. Ibid., 253–54. A more reasonable objection to Mill's position, James implies, is that many marriages may be dissolved if they are based purely on affection rather than on egotism and self-sacrifice.

41. Myers, *William James*, 426.

42. "The Strenuous Life," in Theodore Roosevelt, *The Strenuous Life* (New York: Century, 1902), 3–4.

43. Henry Adams, *The Education of Henry Adams*, ed. Ernest Samuels (1918; reprint, Boston: Houghton Mifflin, 1974), 505. See also 379–90.

44. "Gospel of Relaxation," in *Talks to Teachers on Psychology* (Cambridge: Harvard University Press, 1983), 117–31; "Vacations," in *Essays, Comments, and Reviews*, 3–7; see also Don Browning, "William James's Philosophy of the Person," *Zygon* 10 (June 1975): 169; Henry D. Aiken, "William James as Moral and Social Philosopher," *Philosophic Exchange* 3 (Summer 1980): 62–63; and Perry, *Thought and Character*, 2:353.

45. "Moral Equivalent of War," 171.

46. *Principles of Psychology*, 2:1022–57.

47. Ibid., 2:1029–33, 1039–43, 1049–55; *The Will to Believe* (1897; reprint, New York: Dover, 1956), 82–83; "Remarks at the Peace Banquet," 121–22; "Robert Gould Shaw: Oration by Professor William James," 72; "Moral Equivalent of War," 164–65, all in *Essays in Religion and Morality*; Robert L. Beisner, *Twelve Against Empire: The Anti-Imperialists, 1898–1900* (New York: McGraw-Hill, 1968), 40, 42; Deborah J. Coon, "Courtship with Anarchy: The Socio-Political Foundations of William James's Pragmatism" (Ph.D. diss., Harvard University, 1988), 168. Although James does not elsewhere write much about political theorists other than Plato and Hegel, his *Principles of Psychology* contains many references to Hobbes's *Leviathan* and Locke's *Essay Concerning Human Understanding*.

48. James's pejorative account of homosexuality can be found in the next paragraph in *Principles of Psychology*, 2:1054–55. But while defending the eternal nature of heterosexual romantic love, he also proclaims: "Friendship exists now as much as it ever did, but we fail to find in it food for the same literary treatment. Young fellows inspire romantic affection still in old fellows' breasts, but the old fellows are a little ashamed of owning to this form of emotional susceptibility now. In ancient times it was the fashion, and they were proud of it" (review of *Romantic Love and Personal Beauty* by Henry T. Finck in *Essays, Comments, and Reviews*, 404).

49. James says that the declaration of war on Spain reflected the problem when

"the excitement of action gets loose. . . . Human Nature is everywhere the same; and at the least temptation all the old military passions rise, and sweep everything before them" (letter to Francois Pillon, 15 June 1898, *Letters of William James,* 2:73–74). See also letter to Frederic Myers, 1 January 1896, in Perry, *Thought and Character,* 2:305, 309–17; "Address on the Philippine Question," in *Essays, Comments, and Reviews,* 85; *Principles of Psychology,* 2:1056–57; *Varieties of Religious Experience,* 374; letter to Flournoy, 17 June 1898, in *The Letters of William James and Theodore Flournoy,* ed. Robert C. Le Clair (Madison: University of Wisconsin Press, 1966), 73; and Coon, "Courtship with Anarchy," 129–32, 149.

50. "Remarks at the Peace Banquet," *Essays in Religion and Morality,* 121; Browning, "William James's Philosophy of the Person," 166–67.

51. *Varieties of Religious Experience,* 214–15.

52. "Moral Equivalent of War," 170. James wrote, "Militarism is the great preserver of our ideals of hardihood, and human life without hardihood would be contemptible ("Moral Equivalent of War," 166)." See also 169 and Myers, *William James,* 441.

53. James's pacifism is revealed in "Moral Equivalent of War," 170. See also "Robert Gould Shaw," 73, and Perry, *Thought and Character* 2:277–78. See also George Fredrickson, *The Inner Civil War: Northern Intellectuals and the Crisis of the Union* (New York: Harper and Row, 1965), 235, and Cotkin, *William James,* 121. James's anti-imperialism can be seen in *Letters of William James and Theodore Flournoy,* 72. He exclaimed in a letter, "God damn the United States for its vile conduct in the Philippine Isles" (quoted in Beisner, *Twelve Against Empire,* 44–45).

54. Jean Bethke Elshtain finds James's formulation a necessary result of liberalism's "binary opposition between war and peace" (*Women and War* [New York: Basic Books, 1987], 230–31). George Cotkin has suggested that James's fondness for the rhetoric of manly heroism was due to the guilt he felt for sitting on the sidelines during the Civil War, the great event of his generation (*William James,* 21, 29, 100–101). Read psychologically, James's call for the moral equivalent of war was an attempt to claim some of the soldier's glory for civilians like himself. R. B. Perry adds that James's "exhortation to action was addressed primarily to himself" because of his periodic depressions (*Thought and Character,* 2:674).

55. *Principles of Psychology:* 1:130. In "Gospel of Relaxation" in *Talks to Teachers,* James wrote: "By regulating the action, which is under the more direct control of the will, we can indirectly regulate the feeling, which is not. . . . There is . . . no better known or more generally useful precept in the moral training of youth or in one's personal self-discipline, than that which bids us pay primary attention to what we do and express, and not to care too much for what we feel" (133). See

also "Moral Equivalent of War," 173–74; "Energies of Men," in *Essays in Religion and Morality*, 136; *Principles of Psychology*, 2:948–49; and Browning, "William James's Philosophy of the Person," 168–69.

56. *Principles of Psychology*, 2:1058, 1077–78, 1080–81, 1085–86. See Gerald E. Myers, "Introduction," in *Talks to Teachers*, xxiii–iv.

57. On the cultural encouragement to violence in the United States, see James William Gibson, *Warrior Dreams: Paramilitary Culture in Post-Vietnam America* (New York: Hill and Wang, 1994).

58. McWilliams points out that societies not only curb destructive feelings but frequently provoke prejudice and violence (editorial comment).

59. *Will to Believe*, 174–75. Of course, some effort to control fate is the essence of politics. Pitkin writes, "What distinguishes politics, as Arendt and Aristotle said, is action—the possibility of a shared, collective, active intervention in our fate, in what would otherwise be the by-product of private decisions" ("Justice," 345; see also 343–45).

60. Letter to H. G. Wells, 11 September 1906, in *Letters of William James*, 2:260; *Varieties of Religious Experience*, 117. One hopes that James's use of two feminine images in referring to success as an enemy does not indicate unconscious misogyny.

61. *Varieties of Religious Experience*, 72, 318; *Talks to Teachers*, 141.

62. Quoted in Lloyd Morris, *William James: Message of a Modern Mind* (New York: Charles Scribner's Sons, 1950), 77.

63. See Plato, "The Apology." James's model presumes democratic institutions that will not allow coercion of the poor when they attempt to act.

64. *Varieties of Religious Experience*, 240–56; *Will to Believe*, 101–2; *Essays in Religion and Morality*, 169–73; *Talks to Teachers*, 172–75, 189.

65. It hurts to walk past a homeless person and to hear the long soliloquies pleading for money in the subway cars just as it is painful to read the stories about and see the pictures of refugees in Bosnia, corpses and survivors hacked by machetes in Haiti, the swollen stomachs of starving children in Somalia, and victims of terrorist bombings, incest, rape, and murder. Although nothing like the suffering of the victims, empathetic pain must also be borne. How could Hegel have found the will of God revealed in the morning newspaper?

66. Oliver Wendell Holmes, "Speech at a Dinner Given by the Bar Association of Boston," 7 March 1900, in *The Occasional Speeches of Justice Oliver Wendell Holmes*, ed. Mark DeWolfe Howe (Cambridge: Harvard University Press, 1962), 122–27.

67. Perry, *Thought and Character*, 2:251.

68. Perry is perplexed by the fact that James criticized in Holmes what "James himself seemed so often to be preaching . . . action for the action's sake" (ibid.).

Perry claimed that James demanded that people "serve . . . a moral ideal," but that is something different.

69. *Talks to Teachers*, 163 (emphasis in original).

70. "Governor Roosevelt's Oration (1899)," in *Essays, Comments, and Reviews*, 163. See Fredrickson, *The Inner Civil War*, 236.

71. Brown, *Manhood and Politics*, 206. She also writes, rather ominously: "Is this a clarion call for the death of politics, of heroism, of striving and glory, of men? No, we must keep them all, relieve them of their pathologies and incorporate into them what they have excluded, repudiated, suppressed, and denied" (187). On the difference between male and female heroism, see Di Stefano, *Configurations of Masculinity*, 99–100.

72. "Certainly there are countless examples of people arguing for the courage of one's convictions, of standing up for the things you believe. It does not always have to do with death. Maybe with Machiavelli it courts death, but that is a very special *condottiere* conception of courage" (Wolin editorial comments).

73. "Moral Equivalent of War," 170.

74. See Hartsock, "Prologue," 142. In "The Apology" and "Crito," Socrates offers a model of being willing to suffer and to die in acting upon one's convictions, which he explicitly claims is based on the heroism of Achilles.

75. *Varieties of Religious Experience*, 214–15.

76. I recognize that the constrictions of gender roles have begun to be loosened only recently, that historically, women have been discouraged from taking full part in sports and combat, and that women's athletics still do not receive the attention and funding equal to that of men. For example, a generation ago women were not allowed to guide rafting trips as often as they are now, and the following comment about the ski industry is applicable to many other sports: "Skiing is a very masculine sport," said Tedann Olsen, an advertising coordinator for a manufacturer of skiing equipment. "Men's racing has been better funded than women's, and the equipment and sales reps are men" (quoted in Barbara Lloyd, "Women Are Courted by Makers of Snow Boards," *New York Times* [11 January 1996], B17).

77. Adams, *The Great Adventure*, links James's suggestions for a moral equivalent of war with feminist efforts to find substitutes for military glory and says that neither caught the imagination of the American public (82). See "Moral Equivalent," 171–72, for a list of possible substitute actions.

78. "Shyness needs to be related to a substantive problem such as those who by temperament or by inclination do not want to take part. Radical democracy does not force people to take part; there's no need for that sort of Rousseauist coercion. Radical democracy is certainly about participation, but supposedly people are rational enough to realize that their interests and concerns are at stake in

what's being decided, and they should take part in their own interests" (Wolin editorial comments).

79. "Moral Equivalent of War," 170 (emphasis added).


## 3. Sources of Respect

1. Quoted in Benjamin DeMott, "The Twentieth Century, 1900–76," in *America in Literature*, vol. 2, ed. Alan Trachtenberg and Benjamin DeMott (New York: John Wiley and Sons, 1978), 808.

2. At least theoretically, the unity produced by mutual respect could produce a strong state and a hegemonic identity.

3. See Michael H. Hunt, *Ideology and U.S. Foreign Policy* (New Haven: Yale University Press, 1987). Prominent recent examples include intrusions into Vietnam, Grenada, Panama, and the Persian Gulf. Recent U.S. interventions in Somalia and Haiti are ambiguous.

4. Steven A. Holmes, "Howard University Postponed Lecture by a Jewish Historian," *New York Times*, 16 April 1994, A9.

5. "Mississippi Town Roiled by Lesbians' Plan for a Women's Camp," *New York Times*, 9 January 1994, sec. 1, p. 14.

6. On veiling and the control of women in "established" Islam, see Leila Ahmed, *Women and Gender in Islam: Historical Roots of a Modern Debate* (New Haven: Yale University Press, 1992), especially 149–55, 220–34, and Peter Steinfels, "Beliefs," *New York Times*, 1 July 1995, sec. 1, p. 10.

7. See William E. Connolly, "The Problem of Evil" and "Responsibility for Evil," in Connolly, *Identity/Difference* (Ithaca: Cornell University Press, 1991), 1–15, 95–122. "The peculiar practices of Islam with respect to women had always formed part of the Western narrative of the quintessential otherness and inferiority of Islam" (Ahmed, *Women and Gender in Islam*, 149).

8. This paragraph was suggested by Wolin.

9. See *Federalist* No. 10 and "The Ghostly Body Politic: *The Federalist* Papers and Popular Sovereignty," in Joshua Miller, *Rise and Fall of Democracy in Early America* (University Park: Pennsylvania State University Press, 1991), 105–29.

10. I will show later that Connolly has apprehensions concerning the responsibility that political community devolves on the citizens.

11. Giles Gunn, *Thinking Across the American Grain* (Chicago: University of Chicago Press, 1992), 37. Arendt also advises that in politics positions should not be advocated as absolute and demands should not be nonnegotiable (see especially Hannah Arendt, "On Humanity in Dark Times: Thoughts About Lessing," in Arendt, *Men in Dark Times* [New York: Harcourt, Brace, and World, 1968], 24–

25). See Sidney Hook, "M & S Attitudes: A Reply," *Social Frontier* 4:32 (February 1938): 156. Wolin cautions that coercion may lurk in the ideal of negotiation: "A politics that is strongly dependent on the practices of negotiation will be perplexed or alarmed by the presence of stubbornly maintained differences and hesitate to extend recognition or do it grudgingly" ("Democracy, Difference, and Re-Cognition," *Political Theory* 21 [August 1993]: 467).

12. Walter Lippmann, "An Open Mind: William James," *Everybody's Magazine* 23 (December 1910): 800–801.

13. W. E. B. Du Bois, *The Education of Black People*, ed. Herbert Aptheker (Amherst: University of Massachusetts Press, 1973), 89.

14. On the domestic front, see John Higham, *Strangers in the Land: Patterns of American Nativism, 1860–1925*, 2d ed. (New York: Atheneum, 1963), 14, 21, 30–33, 68–72, 120–22, 144, and Harold Faulkner, *Politics, Reform, and Expansion: 1890–1900* (New York: Harper, 1959), 163–84. For a similar concern with cultural diversity by one of James's contemporaries, see William Graham Sumner, *Folkways* (Boston: Ginn and Company, 1907).

15. Frank Lentricchia, in *Ariel and the Police* (Madison: University of Wisconsin Press, 1988), posits that pragmatism developed out of James's anti-imperialist activity (112). On the historical background of American imperialism, see Higham, *Strangers in the Land*, 144; Richard E. Welch, Jr., *Response to Imperialism* (Chapel Hill: University of North Carolina Press, 1979), 8–33; Frederick Merk, *Manifest Destiny and Mission* (New York: Vintage, 1963), 234–65; and Walter LaFeber, *The New Empire: An Interpretation of American Expansion, 1860–1898* (Ithaca: Cornell University Press, 1963). On American opposition to imperialism, including that of James, see Robert L. Beisner, *Twelve Against Empire: The Anti-Imperialists, 1898–1900* (New York: McGraw-Hill, 1968), especially 38–48.

16. Letter to Theodore Flournoy, 17 June 1898, in Ralph Barton Perry, *The Thought and Character of William James*, 2 vols. (Boston: Little, Brown, 1935), 2:307. In a footnote at the bottom of that page, James despairs: "The worst of it is the complete destruction of the old belief in the *vox populi*. There is no doubt of collective attacks of genuine madness over peoples and stampeding them."

17. James to Mrs. Henry Whitman, 5 October 1899, *Letters of William James*, ed. Henry James, 2 vols. (Boston: Atlantic Monthly Press, 1920), 2:105. McWilliams asks if James would have written these words a hundred years later—after the crimes of Hitler, Stalin, and the Khmer Rouge, which involved deadly regimes destroying large numbers of their own people (editorial comment). Wolin responds: "James's argument is not so much an embarrassment because of Hitler, Stalin, and the Khmer Rouge but because it is a continuation of nine-

teenth-century concepts of national self-determination and a forerunner of Wilsonianism. In the next quotation James uses the word 'harmlessly,' indicating that the type of national self-determination that he is willing to defend is not aggressive and genocidal" (editorial comment).

18. "On a Certain Blindness in Human Beings," in *Talks to Teachers on Psychology* (Cambridge: Harvard University Press, 1983), 149. Note that here the solution is to admit that you cannot understand other cultures. Elsewhere James seems to think that you can understand cultures other than your own.

19. "Robert Gould Shaw: Oration by Professor William James," in *Essays in Religion and Morality* (Cambridge: Harvard University Press, 1982), 74. See also *Letters of William James*, 1:252. The problem is that James calls for respecting not only one's opponents but also the established rules of the game. What if the rules institutionalize inequality and thus themselves conflict with the respect principle?

20. This insight comes from Wolin.

21. Adam Gopnick, "Read All About It," *New Yorker*, 12 December 1994, 98.

22. *Talks to Teachers*, 150; emphasis added.

23. W. Y. P. Elliott, *The Pragmatic Revolt in Politics* (New York: Macmillan, 1928), 47. In the Jamesian spirit, Robert Dawidoff writes, "Democracy requires that one have a certain elemental sympathy with what other people think they want" (*The Genteel Tradition* [Chapel Hill: University of North Carolina Press, 1992], 196).

24. Wolin editorial comments.

25. *The Politics of Aristotle*, ed. and trans. Ernest Barker (New York: Oxford University Press, 1946), 129–32.

26. "What Makes a Life Significant," in *Talks to Teachers*, 158–59.

27. Ibid., 159.

28. *Karl Marx: Early Writings*, trans. and ed. T. B. Bottomore (New York: McGraw-Hill, 1963), 12 (emphasis in original).

29. "Would you go so far as to say one should go further than not punishing people for their ideas or not thinking about what they are say? Does one also have an obligation not to promote political, social, or economic policies that will, in effect, serve to eradicate that idea or make it difficult to hold for practical reasons?" (Wolin editorial comments).

30. *The Prism of the Self: Philosophical Essays in Honor of Maurice Natanson*, ed. Steven Galt Crowell (Boston: Kluwer Academic Publishers, 1995), 301 (emphasis in original).

31. Martin Luther King, Jr., "Facing the Challenge of a New Age," in King, *I Have a Dream*, ed. James Melvin Washington (New York: Harper San Francisco, 1992), 21.

32. Christopher Lasch, with Jeffrey Isaac, "Modernity and Progress: An Exchange," *Salmagundi* 93 (Winter 1992): 107.

33. McWilliams asks if these very terms are laden with disrespect (editorial comment). Certainly, they are based on social standards that others are judged not to have met. Can one remain respectful while saying, "That guy never did much with his career," or must one, to be respectful, make no judgment, or go even further and find something to admire in the man?

34. Mickey Kaus, *The End of Equality* (New York: HarperCollins, Basic Books: 1995), quotation and statement are from pp. 161, 163.

35. In a wonderful passage too lengthy to quote here, John Stuart Mill described his father as a model politician, in this characteristic at least, because although he disliked his adversaries, as activists are wont to do, he was fair-minded enough to acknowledge the good points in his opponents' characters and positions (*Autobiography*, ed. John Robson [New York: Penguin, 1990], 57).

36. "Mandela and De Klerk: Words on a Transition," *New York Times*, 3 May 1994, A15. What led Mandela to give this gracious speech? Perhaps it was the strength of his character, an educational influence, de Klerk's virtues, and a pragmatic assessment of the consequences of revenge.

37. Some political activists believe that academics are contemptibly weak when they try to understand and speak moderately about their opponents and that moving people politically requires fervid, unbalanced rhetoric. The second point may be true.

38. In *Men in Dark Times*, Arendt uses different terms to indicate a generosity beyond toleration. "This has very little to do with tolerance in the ordinary sense . . . but it has a great deal to do with the gift of friendship, and with openness to the world, and finally with genuine love of mankind" (26).

39. On toleration generally, see Ingrid E. Creppell, "The Genesis of Toleration as a Value" (Ph.D. diss., University of Chicago, 1994). Admittedly, James's examples of overcoming blindness are about acquiring a new point of view toward other cultures, not studying them.

40. This sentence and the previous one were suggested by Wolin.

41. *Talks to Teachers*, 165–66. Violence and the reconciliation of labor and management were central themes of political and religious theorists in the 1880s. Although James shared with "social Christians" a belief in social harmony and dialogue, along with a critique of capitalism's excesses, he did not put organized religion at the center of his thinking about how to improve understanding between classes. See Andrew Feffer, *The Chicago Pragmatists and American Progressivism* (Ithaca: Cornell University Press, 1993), 67–116. Nor did James share socialists' faith that redistribution of the wealth would end all major conflict.

42. *Talks to Teachers*, 133–34.

43. James Agee, *Let Us Now Praise Famous Men* (Boston: Houghton Mifflin Company, 1941).

44. I discuss the relationship of truth and action in Chapter 4.

45. *Talks to Teachers*, 132–33. Although I agree with James that reason is not the root of most opinions, I would place greater emphasis on personal and cultural influences, e.g., the groups into which one is born, the influential people one encounters.

46. For a discussion of parochialism and democracy in the context of early American politics, see Miller, *Rise and Fall of Democracy*, 100–103.

47. James also contemplated leaving the United States because he so hated the "sight of my fellow beings at hotels and dining-cars having their boiled eggs bro't to them, broken by a negro, two in a cup, and eaten with butter. How irrational this dislike is, is proved both by the logic, and by the pleasure taken in the custom by the elite of mankind over here" (letter to Henry James, 3 May 1903, in *William and Henry, 1897–1910*, vol. 3 of *The Correspondence of William James*, ed. Ignas K. Skrupskelis and Elizabeth M. Berkeley [Charlottesville: University Press of Virginia, 1994], 233).

48. *Talks to Teachers*, 154–56; quotation is on 154.

49. In this way among others, James's critical political position is different from that of Richard Rorty, who invokes pragmatism to justify, even celebrate, existing American values and arrangements.

50. One illustration of what James rejected is John Locke's implied dictum that cultures which do not productively use the land deserve to lose it. "God gave the world . . . to the use of the industrious and rational" (Locke, *Second Treatise of Government*, chap. 5, par. 34).

51. *Talks to Teachers*, 141.

52. Ibid., 146–47.

53. Dewey endorsed this outlook and adopted James's proposal of the school as the site for learning about other cultures and imparting the temperament for civilly discussing differences. See *Democracy and Education*, vol. 9 of *The Middle Works of John Dewey, 1899–1924*, ed. Jo Ann Boydston (Carbondale: Southern Illinois University Press, 1985), 14–28.

54. *Talks to Teachers*, 154–56. On this passage, see George Cotkin, *William James, Public Philosopher* (Baltimore: Johns Hopkins University Press, 1990), 110. On Tolstoy's influence on James, see Deborah J. Coon, "Courtship with Anarchy: The Socio-Political Foundations of William James's Pragmatism" (Ph.D. diss., Harvard University, 1988), 235.

55. *Talks to Teachers*, 133. Here the problem is too much distance, but else-

where James urges us to realize that from a large distance, our differences are insignificant.

56. "The spectator has a long history in philosophy of detachment, distance, and therefore of impartiality and objectivity. James is attacking a position that is virtually identical with the history of philosophy. Today, Foucault and others attack 'the ocular position' " (Wolin editorial comments).

57. *Talks to Teachers*, 151 (emphasis in original). James overlooks the possibility of blindness to the faults in what one loves. Applied to politics, this oversight might take the form of so much devotion to a cause that one becomes unable to perceive in it danger, mistakes, or futility.

58. Like James, Adam Smith believed that true sympathy for others is difficult, but he claimed that it is easier to sympathize with the joyful person than with the sorrowful, which would indicate that we would shun the indigent, ill, and needy (Adam Smith, *The Theory of Moral Sentiments* [Indianapolis: Liberty Classics, 1976], 103–11).

59. Connolly, *Identity/Difference*, x, 178.

60. Ibid., 178. Connolly sees a hostility in identity-creation that may not be intrinsic to it, i.e., one could imagine perceiving differences without the response of envy and fear.

61. Alfred J. Kolatch, *The Jewish Book of Why* (Middle Village, N.Y.: Jonathan David Publishers, 1981), 7.

62. Ambiguity in establishing identity can be painful in a society that requires clear definitions: children of parents who have different racial, religious, or national identities than those of their community lose the comfort of simple solidarity.

63. Connolly, *Identity/Difference*, x, 179.

64. Ibid., 178.

65. Although I do know a man who nostalgically remembers the late Richard J. Daley, mayor of Chicago, because opposition to Daley gave the man a sense of purpose he missed later when fighting more ambiguous targets.

66. Connolly, *Identity/Difference*, 193. See Connolly's critique of Richard Rorty in "Review Symposium on Richard Rorty," *History of the Human Sciences* 3 (February 1990): 108.

67. John H. Schaar, "The Case for Patriotism," in Schaar, *Legitimacy in the Modern State* (New Brunswick, N.J.: Transaction Press, 1981), 291.

68. Ibid., 293. Longtime readers of Schaar's work might find his embrace of the Declaration of Independence ironic because throughout his essays (collected in *Legitimacy in the Modern State*) he criticizes such principles as independence, the document's implied definition of equality, and the pursuit of hap-

piness while he advocates non-Jeffersonian principles of community, tradition, and memory.

69. This was one of the first conundrums I confronted in political theory when I discovered Rousseau in Schaar's class in 1974. I told him that Rousseau's model city in *The Social Contract* would exclude its eccentric creator. Schaar said, "You should decide whether that question really matters, and if you say yes, then you should confront it seriously, thinking about it day and night for at least a year. At the end of that time you will have to ask yourself, 'Am I with Rousseau or against him?' I have done that, and I have decided that I stand with him."

70. Randolph Bourne, another important voice in this conversation, said that Americans need to learn to respect other cultures rather than requiring those cultures to abandon their particular identities in order to adopt an "American identity." Bourne taught that American life would be richer if immigrants preserved what was best in the culture they brought to the United States (see "Transnational America," in Randolph Bourne, *The Radical Will*, ed. Olaf Hansen [New York: Urizen, 1977], 248–64). Like Lincoln, James emphasized obedience to the laws. In a passage cited earlier, lawbreakers would not benefit from James's famous tolerance ("Robert Gould Shaw," 74). Yet, influenced by Darwin's model of evolution, James wrote in *Will to Believe* that geniuses and their followers must transgress the laws to create new systems of belief and institutions (216–54). No less horrified by lynching than was Lincoln, James was more sanguine about the possibility of radical change.

71. *The Portable Abraham Lincoln*, ed. Andrew Delbanco (New York: Penguin, 1993), 22 (emphasis in original).

72. Elaine Thomas notes that in Lincoln's formulation the people do a fair measure of preaching, enforcing, and sacrificing on behalf of the national covenant.

73. Schaar, "The Case for Patriotism," 296.

74. I do not mean to imply that a common belief of the American citizenry in equality, self-government, and mutual respect is something to belittle.

75. Alexis de Tocqueville, *Democracy in America*, ed. J. P. Mayer, trans. George Lawrence (Garden City, N.Y.: Doubleday, 1969), 236, 510; Mary Parker Follett, *The New State: Group Organization the Solution of Popular Government* (1918; reprint, Gloucester, Mass.: Peter Smith, 1965); Hannah Arendt, *The Human Condition* (Chicago: University of Chicago Press, 1958), 58.

76. J. Anthony Lukas portrays this transformation particularly well in *Common Ground* (New York: Random, 1986), the story of three families involved in a clash in Boston over school busing.

77. Follett, *The New State*, 25, 39. This goal is obviously more difficult on the

international level, but various exchange programs for students, teachers, and government leaders in which the languages, history, and customs of other cultures are taught may do some good.

78. Schaar, "The Case for Patriotism," 296.

79. For example, Christine Di Stefano criticizes Mill's theory of tolerance on several grounds, including that of missing the tie between ideas and interests (*Configurations of Masculinity: A Feminist Perspective on Modern Political Theory* [Ithaca: Cornell University Press, 1991], 169).

80. Rousseau, *The Social Contract*, bk. 2, chap. 11, n.1.

81. Norman Jacobson, *Pride and Solace: The Functions and Limits of Political Theory* (New York: Methuen, 1978).

82. Benedict Anderson, *Imagined Communities: Reflections on the Origin and Spread of Nationalism* (New York: Verso, 1991).

## 4. Faith and Doubt

1. One might say that the Soviet Union stands as a counterexample of the benign effects of humanism because atheism did not undermine the ferocity of Soviet communism. But, obviously, communism was based not on pragmatic humanism but on fervent faith in Marx and Engels, Lenin and Stalin, and dialectical materialism.

2. *Pragmatism and the Meaning of Truth* (Cambridge: Harvard University Press, 1975), 290.

3. Ibid., 125.

4. *Talks to Teachers on Psychology* (Cambridge: Harvard University Press, 1983), 165–66. Wolin comments: "In thinking about James here, I am reminded of Charles Taylor's argument that you should always try deal with opponents by showing their case at its strongest, not by winning debater's points against them. This takes James's point one step further" (editorial comments).

5. Wolin editorial comments.

6. For Follett, see Chapter 3.

7. James to Dickson S. Miller, 30 August 1896, in *Letters of William James*, ed. Henry James, 2 vols. (Boston: Atlantic Monthly Press, 1920), 2:49–50. Two types of actors, one acting on a "monist" model, the other on a "pluralistic" one, are described by James in "The Absolute and the Strenuous Life," in *Pragmatism and the Meaning of Truth*, 289–91.

8. Henry Adams, *The Education of Henry Adams*, ed. Ernest Samuels (Boston: Houghton Mifflin, 1974).

9. For an elaboration of the concept of "pluralist universe," see James, "A

Pluralistic Universe," in *The Writings of William James*, ed. John J. McDermott (Chicago: University of Chicago Press, 1977).

10. *Pragmatism and the Meaning of Truth*, 116.

11. "Pragmatism and Religion," in *Pragmatism and the Meaning of Truth*, 131–44.

12. *The Will to Believe* (1897; reprint, New York: Dover, 1956), 3, 184.

13. James discussed his model of change most extensively in "The Dilemma of Determinism," in *Will to Believe*, 145–83. For an exploration of the meaning of "success" in politics, see Joshua Miller, "No Success Like Failure: Existential Politics in Norman Mailer's *The Armies of the Night*," *Polity* 22 (Spring 1990): 379–96.

14. Ralph Barton Perry, *The Thought and Character of William James*, 2 vols. (Boston: Little, Brown, 1935), 1:488.

15. *Varieties of Religious Experience* (Cambridge: Harvard University Press, 1985), 219–20.

16. Ibid., 272.

17. See Sacvan Bercovitch, *The American Jeremiad* (Madison: University of Wisconsin Press, 1978).

18. Brian Wiener points out that Jefferson can be read in a Jamesian fashion if "holding" the truths is interpreted as "choose to believe" rather than "we know without having to prove it that our American view is that of God" (editorial comment).

19. *The Federalist* (New York: Modern Library, n.d.), 3.

20. Perry, *Thought and Character*, 2:277.

21. Wolin editorial comments.

22. Henry S. Commager, *The American Mind* (New Haven: Yale University Press), 83.

23. Gay Wilson Allen, *William James: A Biography* (New York: Viking, 1967), 161–70. See also George Cotkin, *William James, Public Philosopher* (Baltimore: Johns Hopkins University Press, 1990), 55–56.

24. "The Will to Believe," in *Pragmatism and the Meaning of Truth*, 125.

25. See Jeffrey Lustig, *Corporate Liberalism* (Berkeley: University of California Press, 1982), 159–63.

26. "Rationality, Activity, and Faith," *Princeton Review* 2 (July 1882): 71.

27. See "What Pragmatism Means," in *Pragmatism and the Meaning of Truth*, 27–44.

28. Niccolo Machiavelli, *The Prince*, trans. and ed. Robert M. Adams (New York: Norton, 1977), chap. 15, p. 44.

29. Flannery O'Connor, Letter to "A.," 27 June 1959, in *The Habit of Being*, ed. Sally Fitzgerald (New York: Farrar, Straus, Giroux, 1979), 338.

30. David W. Blight, *Frederick Douglass' War: Keeping Faith in Jubilee* (Baton Rouge: Louisiana State University Press, 1989), 11.

31. On Wells's career, see Paula Giddings, *When and Where I Enter* (New York: William Morrow, 1984), 17–31.

32. Martin Luther King, Jr., "Letter from a Birmingham Jail," in King, *I Have a Dream: Twenty-Four Writings and Speeches That Changed the World*, ed. James Melvin Washington (New York: Harper San Francisco, 1992), 98.

33. The religious sources of the civil rights movement are explored in Taylor Branch, *Parting the Waters* (New York: Simon and Schuster, 1989).

34. See Gordon S. Wood, *The Creation of the American Republic* (Chapel Hill: University of North Carolina Press, 1969), 344–564.


5. Democratic Teaching

1. The problem of silence is not unique to universities in the 1990s. Describing Harvard in 1871 Henry Adams wrote: "The only privilege a student had that was worth his claiming was that of talking to the professor, and the professor was bound to encourage it. His only difficulty on that side was getting them to talk at all. He had to devise schemes to find what they were thinking about, and induce them to risk criticism from their fellows. Any large body of students stifles the student. No man can instruct more than half-a-dozen students at once. The whole problem of education is one of its cost in money" (Henry Adams, *The Education of Henry Adams*, ed. Ernest Samuels [1918; reprint, Boston: Houghton Mifflin, 1974], 302).

2. David Mamet powerfully explores these issues in his play *Oleanna* (New York: Vintage, 1993).

3. *Karl Marx: Early Writings*, trans. and ed. T. B. Bottomore (New York: McGraw-Hill, 1963), 124–25.

4. "If that is supposed to sum up what has gone before, it is more than a feeling of power. I would assume that James is proposing actual institutional arrangements that would give the students actual power" (Wolin editorial comments).

5. Richard Hofstadter, *Anti-Intellectualism in American Life* (New York: Vintage, 1963).

6. Michel Foucault, *Discipline and Punish*, trans. Alan Sheridan (New York: Pantheon, 1977).

7. In addition to *Talks to Teachers*, James wrote several essays on education, including "The True Harvard" (74–77), "Stanford's Ideal Destiny" (102–6), and "The Social Value of the College-Bred" (106–12), all of which are contained in

William James, *Essays, Comments, and Reviews* (Cambridge: Harvard University Press, 1987). Although John Dewey's writings on education are more familiar today, Dewey acknowledged James had an important influence upon his own thinking. See Jo-Anna Johnson Moore, "William James and Art: Perspectives for Art Educators" (Ph.D. diss., Harvard University, 1991), 3–4; Frederick E. Bolton, "Great Contributions to Education: 1. William James," *Progressive Education* 7:3 (1930): 82–87; and Bird T. Baldwin, "William James's Contributions to Education," *Journal of Educational Psychology* 2 (1911): 369–82.

8. Paul F. Boller, Jr., "William James as Educator: Individualism and Democracy," *Teachers College Record* 80:3 (1979): 587–601.

9. Gay Wilson Allen, *William James* (New York: Viking, 1967), 305. "This story does not show James to be democratic. It suggests that he was arbitrary—indulgent (if understandably) toward Stein and unfair to students who did the work. In fact, it indicates his elitism: he made the very able Stein above the law, a favorite preferred to her peers. Neither he nor Stein submitted to the judgment of the community" (McWilliams editorial comment).

10. Ralph Barton Perry, *The Thought and Character of William James*, 2 vols. (Boston: Little, Brown, 1935), 2:695–96.

11. James believed in teaching subjects historically so that human effort and will would be appreciated. Colleges should teach "biographical history, not that of politics merely, but of anything and everything so far as human efforts and conquests are factors that have played their part" ("Social Value of the College-Bred," 108). See also Gerald E. Myers, "Introduction" in *Talks to Teachers*, xix.

12. *Talks to Teachers*, 106. "The mind of him whose fields of consciousness are complex, and who, with the reasons for the action, see the reasons against it, and yet, instead of being palsied, acts in a way that takes the whole field into consideration—so, I say, is such a mind the ideal sort of mind that we should seek to reproduce in our pupils" (ibid.).

13. Ibid. James saw the typical southerner as all action, the northerner as all inhibition.

14. Ibid., 50.

15. *Talks to Teachers*, 30, 32. James asserted, "You should regard your professional task as if it consisted chiefly and essentially in *training the pupil to behavior*" (26). He defined education as "the organization of acquired habits of conduct and tendencies to behavior" (27). Habits lead to destiny, and education changes habits. "The teacher's prime concern should be to ingrain into the pupil that assortment of habits that shall be most useful to him through life. Education is for behavior, and the habits are the stuff of which behavior consists" (48).

16. Ibid., 68. "You must simply work your pupil into such a state of interest in

what you are going to teach him that every other object of attention is banished from his mind; then reveal it to him so impressively that he will remember the occasion to his dying day; and finally fill him with a devouring curiosity to know what the next steps in connection with the subject are" (16). See also 73, 83, 107, and Myers, "Introduction," xix–xxiii.

17. The tone of college work, James said, should be adult and professional ("The Proposed Shortening of the College Course," in *Essays, Comments, and Reviews*, 40).

18. Ibid. and "Concerning Student Celebrations and Self-Government," in *Essays, Comments, and Reviews*, 124. "I feel, as do my colleagues, that the sense of responsibility comes with freedom, and that a Harvard student can feel no greater challenge to his self control and control of others than when he realizes that the repute and safety of the college yard are committed entirely to his hands" (123).

19. William James, *Some Problems of Philosophy* (Cambridge: Harvard University Press, 1979), xxi, 11.

20. He wrote in *Some Problems of Philosophy*, "If the best use of our colleges is to give young men a wider openness of mind and a more flexible way of thinking than special technical training can generate, then we hold that philosophy (taken in the broad sense . . . ) is the most important of all college studies." The goal of philosophy may not be to find universal truth, but "one can never deny that philosophic study means the habit of always seeing an alternative, of not taking the usual for granted, of making conventionalities fluid again, of imagining foreign states of mind. In a word, it means the possession of mental perspective." He said that students should get from their teachers, not doctrines, but "the living, philosophic attitude of mind, the independent personal look at all the data of life, and the eagerness to harmonize them" (4–5).

21. Ibid., 10–11; see also "The True Harvard," 76.

22. "Great Men and Their Environment," in *The Will to Believe* (1897; reprint, New York: Dover, 1956, 229.

23. "Social Value of the College-Bred," 109.

24. "Stanford's Ideal Destiny," 104.

25. "Social Value of the College-Bred," 109–10.

26. Wolin editorial comments.

27. " 'Do people truly deprived of the knowledge of each thing that *is,* who lack a distinct pattern of it in their souls, who are unable to look at absolute truth like painters and constantly refer to it over there and contemplate it as accurately as possible, and then either set up standards here, if they must, of beauty, justice, and goodness, or guard and preserve the existing ones—do people like that seem better than blind men? . . . Then shall we make guardians them, or the ones who

. . . have also recognized each thing that *is?*' " (Plato, *The Republic*, ed. and trans. Raymond Larson [Arlington Heights, Ill.: Harlan Davidson, 1979], 484c–d, 147).

28. See "What Makes a Life Significant," in *Talks to Teachers*, 150–67.

29. Plato, *Republic*, bk. 4, 435e–442d, 102–9.

30. See Sheldon S. Wolin, "Political Philosophy and Philosophy," in *Politics and Vision: Continuity and Innovation in Western Political Thought* (Boston: Little, Brown, 1960), 1–27; Wolin, "Political Theory as a Vocation," in *Machiavelli and the Nature of Political Thought*, ed. M. Fleisher (New York: Atheneum, 1972), 23–75; and Wolin, *Hobbes and the Epic Tradition of Political Theory* (Los Angeles: Clark Memorial Library, University of California, 1970).

31. *Talks to Teachers*, 13. The intellectual influence would even extend to other nations, although James does not claim that Americans invented the intellectual temperament. Universities should "mediat[e] between America and Asia . . . helping the more intellectual men of both continents to understand each other better" ("Stanford's Ideal Destiny," 106).

32. "The Proposed Shortening of the College Course," 36. James wrote in his essay on "The Ph.D. Octopus" that the sole aim of graduate school should be to increase the number of learned people (*Essays, Comments, and Reviews*, 70). See also "Stanford's Ideal Destiny," 104, and *Will to Believe*, 260–61.

33. "Proposed Shortening of the College Course," 37.

34. Ibid., 37, 38, 35.

35. Democratic colleges should have the widest possible influence, James believed. The more people who came into contact with the college-educated the better it would be for the country.

36. *Talks to Teachers*, 13.

37. "Social Value of the College-Bred," 110.

38. "Stanford's Ideal Destiny," 104 (emphasis in original).

39. "Proposed Shortening of the College Course," 37.

40. "Social Value of the College-Bred," 111. "If we are to be the yeast-cake for democracy's dough, if we are to make it rise with culture's preferences, we must see to it that culture spreads broad sails. We must shake the old double reefs out of the canvas into the wind and sunshine, and let in every modern subject, sure that any subject will prove humanistic, if its setting be kept only wide enough" (110).

41. "Social Value of the College-Bred," 108; "Proposed Shortening of the College Course," 34.

42. "Stanford's Ideal Destiny," 105. College should teach "the sense for human superiority" ("Social Value of the College-Bred," 108).

43. "Social Value of the College-Bred," 107. "In picking out from history our heroes, and communing with their kindred spirits . . . each one of us may best

fortify and inspire what creative energy may lie in his own soul" ("The Importance of Individuals," *Will to Believe*, 260–61).

44. Wolin editorial comments.

45. "Social Value of the College-Bred," 108.

46. Letter to H. G. Wells, 11 September 1906, in *Letters of William James*, ed. Henry James, 2 vols. (Boston: Atlantic Monthly Press, 1920), 2:260.

47. "Social Value of the College-Bred," 110.

48. See Henry Adams, *Degradation of the Democratic Dogma* (New York: Harper and Row, 1919).

49. "Social Value of the College-Bred," 109.

50. Ibid., 106. "The great problem is to make our colleges tell in our national life: the leaders of every generation should as far as possible be college-bred men. Now college breeding doesn't by itself make leaders; leaders are made by natural ability and force. But the colleges ought so to cast their net that few young fellows of ability and force escape their toils" ("Proposed Shortening of the College Course," 38).

51. *Talks to Teachers*, 70.

52. Ibid., 68.

53. Ibid., 71–72.

54. Ibid., 30.

55. Adams, *Education of Henry Adams*, 300.


Conclusion

1. Hannah Arendt, *Totalitarianism* (New York: Harcourt, Brace and World, 1951), 3–38.

2. *The Oxford English Dictionary*, s.v., "temperament."

3. Alexis de Tocqueville, *Democracy in America*, ed. J. P. Mayer, trans. George Lawrence (Garden City, N.Y.: Doubleday, 1969), 189, 243.

4. "Isn't this solution a little too easy? Doesn't it cut across the whole thrust of capitalist understandings of firms and organizations? One has to face up to the antidemocratic character of many of the institutions in the society, of which the school and the workplace are only two—most important perhaps, but only two. If you're going to advocate a democratic citizenry, you are going to have to be much more critical and expect much more. You will have to understand not only those who disagree with you but those who have a power which they would feel is threatened by the sort of formulations you are making here. This points to a problem in James. Does he come to terms or even recognize the difficulty of action in a hierarchical, institutional setting of the kind that you

describe? Does he not tend to presume most of the time a kind of debating society conception of political disagreement?" (Wolin editorial comments). In Chapters 1 and 3, I showed that James, while not concentrating on institutional analysis, was sensitive to the threat large, bureaucratic institutions posed to the type of citizenship he was attempting to develop in Americans.

5. I provide the bibliographic information about this revival in the section "Suggested Reading."

6. Dewey, *Democracy and Education,* vol. 9 of *The Middle Works of John Dewey, 1899–1924,* ed. Jo Ann Boydston (Carbondale: Southern Illinois University Press, 1985), 25–26, 104–5.

7. Ibid., 227–33, 292, 298, and Dewey, *Reconstruction in Philosophy and Essays,* vol. 12 of *The Middle Works* (Carbondale: Southern Illinois University Press, 1988), chaps. 1–3.

8. Richard Rorty, *Contingency, Irony, Solidarity* (New York: Cambridge University Press, 1989), 198.

9. Richard Rorty, *Objectivity, Relativism, and Truth,* vol. 1 of *Philosophical Papers* (New York: Cambridge University Press, 1991), 198, 213, 110.

10. Cornel West, *The American Evasion of Philosophy: A Genealogy of Pragmatism* (Madison: University of Wisconsin Press, 1989), 54–68.

11. Cornel West, *Keeping Faith: Philosophy and Race in America* (New York: Routledge, 1993), 28, 140; 29, 291; 113.

12. Ibid., xi, 27, 89, 103; 139; 95.

13. Ibid., 135, 139.

14. *Pragmatism* (Cambridge: Harvard University Press, 1975), 14.

# SUGGESTED READING

Students of politics or political theory might well begin to encounter James through his essays "On a Certain Blindness in Human Beings" and "What Makes a Life Significant" in *Talks to Teachers on Psychology and to Students on Some of Life's Ideals* (Cambridge: Harvard University Press, 1983; New York: Norton, 1958). Then peruse *Pragmatism* (Cambridge: Harvard University Press, 1975), *The Will to Believe* (Cambridge: Harvard University Press, 1975; New York: Dover, 1956), and *Varieties of Religious Experience* (Cambridge: Harvard University Press, 1985; New York: Vintage Books, Library of America, 1990). Finally, selectively study his wonderful two-volume masterpiece *The Principles of Psychology* (Cambridge: Harvard University Press, 1981; New York: Dover, 1890). Scholars will want to use the Harvard University Press editions of *The Works of William James;* everyone else will appreciate less-expensive paperbacks. John J. McDermott's collection of *The Writings of William James* (Chicago: University of Chicago Press, 1977) is handy.

Crucial James essays include "Robert Gould Shaw," "Remarks at the Peace Banquet," "The Energies of Men," and "The Moral Equivalent of War," all in *Essays in Religion and Morality* (Cambridge: Harvard University Press, 1982). Other important pieces, including "Vacations," "The Proposed Shortening of the College Course," "The Ph.D. Octopus," "The True Harvard," "Address on the Philippine Question," "Thomas Davidson: Individualist," "Stanford's Ideal Destiny," and "The Social Value of the College-Bred," appear in *Essays, Comments, and Reviews* (Cambridge: Harvard University Press, 1987). In that same volume, read the letters to the editor on disorders in the college yard, the Philippines, and lynching. The review of *Women's Suffrage* by Horace Bushnell and *The Subjection of Women* by John Stuart Mill in *Essays, Comments, and Reviews*, 246–56, is James's most extended comment on feminism.

James expressed many of his ideas most clearly in his letters. A selection

155

of these are found in *Letters of William James*, 2 vols., ed. Henry James (Boston: Atlantic Monthly Press, 1920), and four volumes have so far appeared of *The Correspondence of William James*, ed. Ignas K. Skrupskelis and Elizabeth M. Berkeley (Charlottesville: University of Virginia Press, 1992–1994). The traditional, and still excellent, starting place for seeing the broad sweep of James's life and ideas is Ralph Barton Perry's *The Thought and Character of William James*, 2 vols. (Boston: Little, Brown, 1935). Perry combines biography, selections from the correspondence, excerpts from James's published writings, and intelligent commentary. James's life and the history of his family are fascinating. Gay Wilson Allen's *William James* (New York: Viking, 1967) is a straightforward biography. R. W. B. Lewis takes on the whole clan in *The Jameses: A Family Narrative* (New York: Farrar, Straus, and Giroux, 1991).

The secondary literature on James is vast, and I cannot claim to have read all of it. For the purposes of discerning James's political ideas I found most useful George Cotkin, *William James, Public Philosopher* (Baltimore: Johns Hopkins University Press, 1990), and Deborah J. Coon, "Courtship with Anarchy: The Socio-Political Foundations of William James's Pragmatism" (Ph.D. diss., Harvard University, 1988). Casey Nelson Blake, a radical democrat, treats James insightfully in *Beloved Community: The Cultural Criticism of Randolph Bourne, Van Wyck Brooks, Waldo Frank, and Lewis Mumford* (Chapel Hill: University of North Carolina Press, 1990). Jeffrey Lustig, in *Corporate Liberalism* (Berkeley: University of California Press, 1982), and Cornel West, in *The American Evasion of Philosophy: A Genealogy of Pragmatism* (Madison: University of Wisconsin Press, 1989), analyze pragmatism from a radical democratic perspective, with incisive treatments of James. James plays an important role in Christopher Lasch, *The True and Only Heaven* (New York: Norton, 1991), in which Lasch applies the categories of *Varieties of Religious Experience* to political actors. C. Wright Mills in *Sociology and Pragmatism*, ed. I. L. Horowitz (New York: Paine-Whitman, 1964), uncovers the political implications of pragmatism and has a good chapter on James. Wilson Carey McWilliams insightfully discusses James in "Old Americans and New," in *The Idea of Fraternity in America* (Berkeley: University California Press, 1973), 473–79.

A classic critique of the political implications of pragmatism, McWilliams's favorite, is W. Y. P. Elliott, *The Pragmatic Revolt in Politics* (New

York: Macmillan, 1928). Elliott was Sheldon Wolin's professor at Harvard, as was R. B. Perry. Although sympathetic to James personally, as are most commentators, Elliott links pragmatism with Georges Sorel on the one side and Mussolini on the other. Richard Hofstadter, in *Social Darwinism in American Thought* (Boston: Beacon, 1955), helpfully elucidates James's critique of social Darwinism. Gerald E. Myers's *William James: His Life and Thought* (New Haven: Yale University Press, 1986) is thorough and helpful for understanding James's politics (see chap. 13, "Morality," 387–445).

One of the best pieces on James is in Josiah Royce, *William James, and Other Essays* (New York: Macmillan, 1911). George Santayana, who invariably speaks of his former teacher with a mixture of respect and condescension, has an essay "William James" in Santayana, *Character and Opinion in the United States* (New York: Scribner's, 1920) and comments on him in *Persons and Places: Fragments of Autobiography*, ed. William G. Holzberger and Herman J. Saatkamp, Jr. (Cambridge, Mass.: MIT Press, 1987). John Dewey frequently wrote about James; one example being "William James in 1926," *New Republic* 47 (30 June 1926): 163–65, and Theodore Roosevelt took a Jamesian theme in a dangerous direction in "The Strenuous Life," in *The Strenuous Life* (New York: Century, 1902), 1–21. Horace Kallen, another student of James and a founder of the New School for Social Research, penned a generous obituary of James in *The Nation* 91 (8 September 1910): 210–21. See also Henry D. Aiken, "William James as Moral and Social Philosopher," *Philosophic Exchange* 3 (Summer 1980): 57–66. George R. Garrison and Edward H. Madden in "William James—Warts and All," *American Quarterly* 29 (Summer 1977): 207–21, harshly judge James's inadequacies as a political actor.

For James's intellectual milieu, see Bruce Kuklick, *The Rise of American Philosophy: Cambridge, Massachusetts, 1860–1930* (New Haven: Yale University Press, 1977), especially the chapter "Social and Political Philosophy," 306–14. W. E. B. Du Bois, *The Souls of Black Folk* (New York: Penguin, 1989), displays James's influence, especially in Du Bois's idea of the talented tenth, corresponding to Jamesian geniuses, who would raise up the masses through reason and vision. I found it instructive to read James as a counterpoint to his friend Henry Adams, especially on the issues of nihilism, action, and gender. See Adams, *The Education of Henry Adams*, ed. Ernest Samuels (Boston: Houghton Mifflin, 1974 [1918]). T. J. Jackson Lears depicts the despair of public intellectuals in *No Place of Grace: An-*

timodernism and the Transformation of American Culture (New York: Pantheon Books, 1981).

For historical context, I found most useful Daniel Schirmer, "William James and the New Age," Science and Society 33 (Fall-Winter 1969): 434–45; Walter LaFeber, The New Empire: An Interpretation of American Expansion, 1860–1898 (Ithaca: Cornell University Press, 1963); Richard E. Welch, Jr., Response to Imperialism (Chapel Hill: University of North Carolina Press, 1979); Robert L. Beisner, Twelve Against Empire: The Anti-Imperialists, 1898–1900 (New York: McGraw-Hill, 1968); Henry Steele Commager, The American Mind (New Haven: Yale University Press, 1950); Frederick Merk, Manifest Destiny and Mission (New York: Vintage, 1963); Harold Faulkner, Politics, Reform, and Expansion: 1890–1900 (New York: Harper, 1959); Michael H. Hunt, Ideology and U.S. Foreign Policy (New Haven: Yale University Press, 1987); and Paula Giddings, When and Where I Enter: The Impact of Black Women on Race and Sex in America (New York: William Morrow, 1984).

On the issue of masculinity and politics, read Wendy L. Brown, Manhood and Politics: A Feminist Reading in Political Theory (Totowa, N.J.: Rowman and Littlefield, 1988); Christine Di Stefano, Configurations of Masculinity: A Feminist Perspective on Modern Political Theory (Ithaca: Cornell University Press, 1991); Nancy C. M. Hartsock, "Prologue to a Feminist Critique of War and Politics," in Women's Views of the Political World of Men, ed. Judith H. Stiehm (Dobbs Ferry, N.Y.: Transnational Publishers, 1984), 121–50; Hanna Fenichel Pitkin, "Justice: On Relating Public and Private," Political Theory 9 (August 1981): 327–52; Sara Evans, Personal Politics: The Roots of Women's Liberation in the Civil Rights Movement and New Left (New York: Vintage, 1980); and Ann Popkin, "The Personal Is Political: The Women's Liberation Movement," in They Should Have Served That Cup of Coffee, ed. Dick Cluster (Boston: South End Press, 1979), 181–224.

For a range of feminist thinking today, see Linda J. Nicholson, ed., Feminism/Postmodernism (New York: Routledge, 1990), and Marianne Hirsch and Evelyn Fox Keller, eds., Conflicts in Feminism (New York: Routledge, 1990). For a blunt attack on James, see Jane Roland Martin, "Martial Virtues or Capital Vices? William James's Moral Equivalent of War Revisited," Journal of Thought 22 (Fall 1987): 32–44. Jean Bethke Elshtain is more subtle in Women and War (New York: Basic Books, 1987). Michael

C. Adams, *The Great Adventure: Male Desire and the Coming of World War I* (Bloomington: Indiana University Press, 1990), describes how men perceived gender roles in the late nineteenth century. For additional insight into the 1890s on several themes, including masculinity, see James C. Malin, *Confounded Rot About Napoleon: Reflections upon Science and Technology, Nationalism, World Depression of the Eighteen-nineties, and Afterwards* (Lawrence, Kans.: James C. Malin, 1961).

When thinking about action, I begin with Machiavelli's *Prince* and then Hannah Arendt's *The Human Condition* (Chicago: University of Chicago Press, 1958). French theorist Georges Sorel (1847–1922) was influenced by James and wrote about him, and Sorel's writings are excerpted and preceded by a masterful introductory essay in *From Georges Sorel: Essays in Socialism and Philosophy*, ed. John L. Stanley, trans. John and Charlotte Stanley (New Brunswick: Transaction Books, 1987). John H. Schaar makes the case for politics and addresses the problem of truth and politics in a contemporary restatement of Machiavelli in his chapter "Power and Purity" in *Legitimacy in the Modern State* (New Brunswick, N.J.: Transaction Books, 1981), 313–30.

Lisa J. Disch pointed me toward an essay by Arendt that articulated precisely what I admire most in James's theory of mutual respect based on plural truths: "On Humanity in Dark Times: Thoughts About Lessing," in *Men in Dark Times* (New York: Harcourt, Brace, and World, 1968), 3–31. I encountered this theme first in William E. Connolly, *Identity/Difference* (Ithaca: Cornell University Press, 1991).

On education, I drew from Jo-Anna Johnson Moore, "William James and Art: Perspectives for Art Educators" (Ph.D. diss., Harvard University, 1991); Paul F. Boller, Jr., "William James as Educator: Individualism and Democracy," *Teachers College Record* 80:3 (1979): 587–601; Frederick E. Bolton, "Great Contributions to Education: 1. William James," *Progressive Education* 7:3 (1930): 82–88; C. Wright Mills, "Social Role of the Intellectual" and "Mass Society and Liberal Education," in *Power, Politics, and People*, ed. I. L. Horowitz (New York: Oxford University Press, 1963); and James McLachlan, "American Colleges and the Transmission of Culture: The Case of the Mugwumps," in Stanley Elkins and Eric McKitrick, eds., *The Hofstadter Aegis* (New York: Knopf, 1974). Merle Curti offers a devastating critique of James and Dewey in *The Social Ideas of American Education* (Patterson, N.J.: Littlefield, Adams and Company, 1959). I caught the spirit of educational innovation from John Andrew Rice, *I Came Out of the Eighteenth Century* (New York: Harper and Brothers, 1942), in which Rice, who founded Black Mountain College, wrote: "Black Mountain was to be education for democracy. . . . If it was to be education for democracy, if that was its end, that must also be its means: it must be education in democracy" (327). His stories about John Dewey ("the only man I have ever known who was completely fit and fitted to live in a democracy" [331]) could almost make you like Dewey.

The tension between progressive education and the movement to make great books the center of the college curriculum deserves further study. Start with the debate between Dewey and Robert Hutchins in *Social Frontier*. Dewey presented "President Hutchins' Proposals to Remake Higher Education," *Social Frontier* 3 (January 1937): 103–4, and Hutchins responded with "Grammar, Rhetoric, and Mr. Dewey," in *Social Frontier* 3 (February 1937): 137–39. They then went at each other a few more times.

The recent interest in pragmatism as democratic politics has centered on Dewey, not James. From the standpoint of democratic thought, Dewey's central works are *The Public and Its Problems* (1927; reprint, Athens, Ohio: Swallow, 1954); *Democracy and Education*, vol. 9 of *The Middle Works of John Dewey, 1899–1924*, ed. Jo Ann Boydston (Carbondale: Southern Illinois University Press, 1985); and *Reconstruction in Philosophy and Essays*, vol. 12 of *The Middle Works*, (1988). See also *Experience and Education* (New York: Macmillan Collier, 1962), and "The Bearings of Pragmatism upon Education," in *The Middle Works*, vol. 4 (1977), 178–91. Democratic theorists will not soon surpass Robert B. Westbrook's lengthy and thorough study, *John Dewey and American Democracy* (Ithaca: Cornell University Press, 1991). Wilson Carey McWilliams writes on Dewey in *The Idea of Fraternity in America* (526–38); Richard Hofstadter, *Anti-Intellectualism in American Life* (New York: Vintage, 1963), is highly critical of James's and Dewey's conceptions of progressive education; and Benjamin Barber draws on Dewey in *Strong Democracy: Participatory Politics for a New Age* (Berkeley: University of California Press, 1984). See also Alan Ryan, *John Dewey and the High Tide of American Liberalism* (New York: W. W. Norton, 1995).

James said Charles S. Peirce invented pragmatism, and he certainly developed a more communitarian epistemology than did James. Peirce's key writings, including "The Fixation of Beliefs" and "How to Make Our Ideas Clear," can be found in *Essential Peirce*, vol. 1, ed. Nathan Houser and Christian Kloesel (Bloomington: Indiana University Press, 1992). See also James Hoopes, "Objectivity and Relativism Affirmed: Historical Knowledge and the Philosophy of Charles S. Peirce," *American Historical Review* 98 (December 1993): 1545–55. Joseph Brent, in *Charles Sanders Peirce: A Life* (Bloomington: Indiana University Press, 1993), portrays a tormented and truly interesting man.

Some books I recognize as being substantial and important, even if I did not draw on them much in this book. Schaar told me as I embarked on this project that I would have to decide if I could possibly add anything to Jacques Barzun's *A Stroll with William James* (New York: Harper and Row, 1983), but I found that Barzun's interests in James almost completely differed from my own with the exception of the chapter "Freedom and Risk," which is concerned with action. Serious scholars of pragmatism and politics should consult James T. Kloppenberg, *Uncertain Victory: Social Democracy and Progressivism in European and American Thought, 1870–1920* (New York: Oxford University Press, 1986); Richard Flathman, *Willful Liberalism: Voluntarism and Individuality in Political Theory and Practice* (Ithaca: Cornell University Press, 1992); Ross Posnock, *The Trial of Curiosity: Henry James, William James, and the Challenge of Modernity* (New York: Oxford University Press, 1991); and John P. Diggins, *The Promise of Pragmatism* (Chicago: University of Chicago Press, 1994). Kloppenberg, Robert B. Westbrook, and James Hoopes review Diggins's book, followed by a reply from Diggins, in the *Intellectual History Newsletter* 17 (1995): 3–30. See also Richard Bernstein, "Dewey, Democracy: The Task Before Us," in *Post-Analytic Philosophy*, ed. John Rajchman and Cornell West (New York: Columbia University Press, 1985).

Richard Rorty is perhaps the key figure in the pragmatist revival, but he wants pragmatism to serve the cause of liberalism, not radical democracy. On the link between philosophy and politics, see pt. 3 of Rorty's *Objectivity, Relativism, and Truth: Philosophical Papers, vol. 1* (New York: Cambridge University Press, 1991), and *Contingency, Irony, Solidarity* (New York: Cambridge University Press, 1989). New works about Rorty are published every week. See the critiques of Rorty by William E. Connolly, "Review Symposium on Richard Rorty," in *History of the Human Sciences* 3 (February 1990): 101–22; Richard Bernstein, "One Step Forward, Two Steps Back," *Political Theory* 15 (November 1987): 538–63; Cornel West, "The Politics of American Neo-Pragmatism," in *Post-Analytic Philosophy*, ed. John Rachjman and Cornel West (New York: Columbia University Press, 1985), 259–75; and Sheldon S. Wolin, "Democracy in the Discourse of Postmodernism," *Social Research* 57 (Spring 1990): 5–30. Rorty's exchange with Clifford Geertz is especially worth reading. Geertz's "Uses of Diversity" appeared in *Michigan Quarterly Review* 25 (1986): 525–34; Rorty's comment, "On Ethnocentrism: A Reply to Clifford Geertz," was published in *Objectivity, Relativism, and Truth*, 203–10.

To explore further the tradition of political theory to which I subscribe, see Sheldon S. Wolin, *Politics and Vision: Continuity and Innovation in Western Political Thought* (Boston: Little, Brown, 1960), Arendt, *The Human Condition*, and Schaar, *Legitimacy in the Modern State*. Although I have not addressed the theme of stream-of-consciousness that James developed in *Principles of Psychology*, and which phenomenologists find crucial, my thinking about James has been informed by existential philosophy. A good place to begin in that subject is Maurice Natanson, *The Journeying Self: A Study in Philosophy and Social Role* (Reading, Mass.: Addison-Wesley, 1970).

# INDEX